AF304005

Defoe Abbott Marx Hardy Machiavelli Montaigne Chesterton Cooper Emerson Joyce Austen Hugo Eliot Grimm
Melville Haggard Molière
Stoker Carroll Christie Maupassant Byron Schiller
Wilde Engels Smith Kafka Hall
Garnett Fitzgerald Einstein Hawthorne
Goethe Dostoyevsky Willis
Cotton Kipling Doyle
Baum Henry Nietzsche
Leslie Dumas Flaubert Turgenev Balzac
Stockton Vatsyayana Crane
Burroughs Verne
Curtis Tocqueville Gogol Vinci
Homer Widger Tolstoy Whitman Busch
Darwin Thoreau Twain Scott Harte
Potter Freud Zola Plato
Kant Jowett Stevenson Dickens Hesse Burton
Andersen Cervantes
London Descartes Voltaire
Poe Aristotle Wells Cooke
Hale James Hastings Irving
Bunner Shakespeare
Richter Chekhov Chambers da Shaw Wodehouse Benedict Alcott
Doré Dante Swift Pushkin Newton

 tredition®

tredition was established in 2006 by Sandra Latusseck and Soenke Schulz. Based in Hamburg, Germany, tredition offers publishing solutions to authors and publishing houses, combined with world-wide distribution of printed and digital book content. tredition is uniquely positioned to enable authors and publishing houses to create books on their own terms and without conventional manufacturing risks.

For more information please visit: www.tredition.com

TREDITION CLASSICS

This book is part of the TREDITION CLASSICS series. The creators of this series are united by passion for literature and driven by the intention of making all public domain books available in printed format again - worldwide. Most TREDITION CLASSICS titles have been out of print and off the bookstore shelves for decades. At tredition we believe that a great book never goes out of style and that its value is eternal. Several mostly non-profit literature projects provide content to tredition. To support their good work, tredition donates a portion of the proceeds from each sold copy. As a reader of a TREDITION CLASSICS book, you support our mission to save many of the amazing works of world literature from oblivion. See all available books at www.tredition.com.

Project Gutenberg

The content for this book has been graciously provided by Project Gutenberg. Project Gutenberg is a non-profit organization founded by Michael Hart in 1971 at the University of Illinois. The mission of Project Gutenberg is simple: To encourage the creation and distribution of eBooks. Project Gutenberg is the first and largest collection of public domain eBooks.

Sermons on Evil-Speaking

Isaac Barrow

Imprint

This book is part of TREDITION CLASSICS

Author: Isaac Barrow
Cover design: Buchgut, Berlin – Germany

Publisher: tredition GmbH, Hamburg - Germany
ISBN: 978-3-8424-2462-3

www.tredition.com
www.tredition.de

INTRODUCTION.

Isaac Barrow was born in London in 1630. His father was draper to the king. His mother died when he was four years old. He was named Isaac after an uncle, who died in 1680, Bishop of St. Asaph. Young Isaac Barrow was educated at the Charterhouse School, and at Felstead, before he went, in 1643, to Cambridge. He entered first at Peterhouse, where his uncle Isaac was a Fellow, but at that time his uncle was ejected from his Fellowship for loyalty to the King's cause, and removed to Oxford; the nephew, who entered at Cambridge, therefore avoided Peterhouse, and went to Trinity College. Young Barrow's father also was at Oxford, where he gave up all his worldly means in service of the King.

The young student at Cambridge did not conceal his royalist feeling, but obtained, nevertheless, a scholarship at Trinity, with some exemptions from the Puritan requirements of subscription. He took his B.A. degree in 1648, and in 1649 was elected to a fellowship of Trinity, on the same day with his most intimate college friend John Ray, the botanist. Ray held in the next year several college offices; was made in 1651 lecturer in Greek, and in 1653 lecturer in Mathematics. Barrow proceeded to his M.A. in 1652, and was admitted to the same degree at Oxford in 1653. In 1654, Dr. Dupont, who had been tutor to Barrow and Ray, and held the University Professorship of Greek, resigned, and used his interest, without success, to get Barrow appointed in his place. Isaac Barrow was then a young man of four-and-twenty, with the courage of his opinions in politics and in church questions, which were not the opinions of those in power.

In 1655 Barrow left Cambridge, having sold his books to raise money for travel. He went to Paris, where his father was with other royalists, and gave some help to his father. Then he went on to Italy, made stay at Florence, and on a voyage from Leghorn to Smyrna stood to a gun in fight with a pirate ship from Algiers that was beaten off. At college and upon his travels Barrow was helped by the liberality of public spirited men who thought him worth their aid. He went on to Constantinople, where he studied the Greek Fathers of the Church; and he spent more than a year in Turkey. He returned through Germany and Holland, reached England in the year before the Restoration, and then, at the age of twenty-nine, he entered holy orders, for which in all his studies he had been preparing.

The Cambridge Greek Professorship, which had before been denied him, was obtained by Barrow immediately after the Restoration. Soon afterwards he was chosen to be Professor of Geometry at Gresham College. In 1663 he preached the sermon in Westminster Abbey at the consecration of his uncle, Isaac, as Bishop of St. Asaph. In that year also he became, at Cambridge, the first Lucasian Professor of Mathematics, for which office he resigned his post at Gresham College.

As Lucasian Professor of Mathematics, Isaac Barrow had among his pupils Isaac Newton. Newton succeeded to the chair in 1669. Barrow resigned because he feared that the duties of the mathematical chair drew his thoughts too much from the duties of the pulpit, towards the full performance of which he had desired all studies to be aids. He was then intent upon the writing of an "Exposition of the Creed, Decalogue, and Sacraments." He held a prebend in Salisbury Cathedral, and a living in Wales, that yielded little for his support after the Professorship had been resigned. But he was one of the King's chaplains, was made D.D. by the King in 1670, and in 1672 he was appointed Master of Trinity by Charles II., who said, when he appointed Isaac Barrow, "that he gave the post to the best scholar in England." Barrow was Vice-Chancellor of the University when he died in 1677, during a visit to London on the business of his college.

The sermons here given were first published in 1678, in a volume entitled "Several Sermons against Evil-speaking." That volume contained ten sermons, of which the publisher said that "the two last, against pragmaticalness and meddling in the affairs of others, do not so properly belong to this subject." The sermons here given follow continuously, beginning with the second in the series. The text of the first sermon was "If any man offend not in word, he is a perfect man." The texts to the last three were: "Speak not evil one of another, brethren;" "Judge not;" and "That ye study to be quiet, and to do your own business."

There were also published in 1678, the year after Barrow's death, a sermon preached by him on the Good Friday before he died, a volume of "Twelve Sermons preached upon several Occasions," and the second edition of a sermon on the "Duty and Reward of Bounty to the Poor." Barrow's works were collected by Archbishop Tillotson, and published, in four folio volumes, in the years 1683-1687. There were other editions in three folios in 1716, in 1722, and in 1741. Dr. Dibdin said of Barrow that he "had the clearest head with which mathematics ever endowed an individual, and one of the purest and most unsophisticated hearts that ever beat in the human breast." In these sermons against Evil Speaking he distinguishes as clearly as Shakespeare does between the playfulness of kindly mirth that draws men nearer to each other and the words that make division. No man was more free than Isaac Barrow from the spirit of unkindness. The man speaks in these sermons. Yet he could hold his own in wit with the light triflers of the court of Charles the Second. It is of him that the familiar story is told of a playful match at mock courtesy with the Earl of Rochester, who meeting Dr. Barrow near the king's chamber bowed low, saying, "I am yours, doctor, to the knee strings." *Barrow* (bowing lower), "I am yours, my lord, to the shoe-tie." *Rochester*: "Yours, doctor, down to the ground." *Barrow*: "Yours, my lord, to the centre of the earth." *Rochester* (not to be out-done): "Yours, doctor, to the lowest pit of hell." *Barrow*: "There, my lord, I must leave you."

Barrow's mathematical power gave clearness to his sermons, which were full of sense and piety. They were very carefully written, copied and recopied, and now rank with the most valued pieces of the literature of the pulpit. He was deeply religious, although he had, besides learning, a lively wit, and never lost the pluck that taught him how to man a gun against a pirate. He was "low of stature, lean, and of a pale complexion," so untidy that on one occasion his appearance in the pulpit is said to have caused half the congregation to go out of church. He gave his whole mind and his whole soul to his work for God. Mythical tales are told of the length of some of his sermons, at a time when an hour's sermon was not considered long. Of one charity-sermon the story is that it lasted three

hours and a half, and that Barrow was requested to print it—"with the other half which he had not had time to deliver." But we may take this tale as one of the quips at which Barrow himself would have laughed very good-humouredly.
H. M.

SERMONS ON EVIL-SPEAKING.

AGAINST FOOLISH TALKING AND JESTING.

"Nor foolish talking, nor jesting, which are not convenient." —Ephes. v.4.

Moral and political aphorisms are seldom couched in such terms that they should be taken as they sound precisely, or according to the widest extent of signification; but do commonly need exposition, and admit exception: otherwise frequently they would not only clash with reason and experience, but interfere, thwart, and supplant one another. The best masters of such wisdom are wont to interdict things, apt by unseasonable or excessive use to be perverted, in general forms of speech, leaving the restrictions, which the case may require or bear, to be made by the hearer's or interpreter's discretion; whence many seemingly formal prohibitions are to be received only as sober cautions. This observation may be particularly supposed applicable to this precept of St. Paul, which seemeth universally to forbid a practice commended (in some cases and degrees) by philosophers as virtuous, not disallowed by reason, commonly affected by men, often used by wise and good persons; from which consequently, if our religion did wholly debar us, it would seem chargeable with somewhat too uncouth austerity and sourness: from imputations of which kind as in its temper and frame it is really most free (it never quenching natural light or cancelling the dictates of sound reason, but confirming and improving them); so it carefully declineth them, enjoining us that "if there be any things" προσφιλη ("lovely," or grateful to men), "any things" ευφημα ("of good report" and repute), "if there be any virtue and any praise" (anything in the common apprehensions of men held worthy and laudable), we should "mind those things," that is, should yield them a regard answerable to the esteem they carry among rational and sober persons.

Whence it may seem requisite so to interpret and determine St. Paul's meaning here concerning *eutrapelia* (that is, facetious speech, or raillery, by our translators rendered "jesting"), that he may consist with himself, and be reconciled to Aristotle, who placeth this practice in the rank of virtues; or that religion and reason may well accord in the case: supposing that, if there be any kind of facetiousness innocent and reasonable, conformable to good manners (regulated by common sense, and consistent with the tenor of Christian duty, that is, not transgressing the bounds of piety, charity, and sobriety), St. Paul did not intend to discountenance or prohibit that kind.

For thus expounding and limiting his intent we have some warrant from himself, some fair intimations in the words here. For first, what sort of facetious speech he aimeth at, he doth imply by the fellow he coupleth therewith; μωρολογια, saith he, η ευτραπελια (foolish talking, or facetiousness): such facetiousness therefore he toucheth as doth include folly, in the matter or manner thereof. Then he further determineth it, by adjoining a peculiar quality thereof, unprofitableness, or impertinency; τα μη ανηκοντα (which are not pertinent), or conducible to any good purpose: whence may be collected that it is a frivolous and idle sort of facetiousness which he condemneth.

But, however, manifest it is that some kind thereof he doth earnestly forbid: whence, in order to the guidance of our practice, it is needful to distinguish the kinds, severing that which is allowable from that which is unlawful; that so we may be satisfied in the case, and not on the one hand ignorantly transgress our duty, nor on the other trouble ourselves with scruples, others with censures, upon the use of warrantable liberty therein.

And such a resolution seemeth indeed especially needful in this our age (this pleasant and jocular age) which is so infinitely addicted to this sort of speaking, that it scarce doth affect or prize anything near so much; all reputation appearing now to veil and stoop to that of being a wit: to be learned, to be wise, to be good, are nothing in comparison thereto; even to be noble and rich are inferior things, and afford no such glory. Many at least (to purchase this glory, to be deemed considerable in this faculty, and enrolled among the wits) do not only make shipwreck of conscience, abandon virtue, and forfeit all pretences to wisdom; but neglect their estates, and prostitute their honour: so to the private damage of many particular persons, and with no small prejudice to the public, are our times possessed and transported with this humour. To repress the excess and extravagance whereof, nothing in way of discourse can serve better than a plain declaration when and how such a practice is allowable or tolerable; when it is wicked and vain, unworthy of a man endued with reason, and pretending to honesty or honour.

This I shall in some measure endeavour to perform.

But first it may be demanded what the thing we speak of is, or what this facetiousness doth import? To which question I might reply as Democritus did to him that asked the definition of a man, "'Tis that which we all see and know": any one better apprehends what it is by acquaintance than I can inform him by description. It is indeed a thing so versatile and multiform, appearing in so many shapes, so many postures, so many garbs, so variously apprehended by several eyes and judgments, that it seemeth no less hard to settle a clear and certain notion thereof, than to make a portrait of Proteus, or to define the figure of the fleeting air. Sometimes it lieth in pat allusion to a known story, or in seasonable application of a trivial saying, or in forging an apposite tale: sometimes it playeth in words and phrases, taking advantage from the ambiguity of their sense, or the affinity of their sound: sometimes it is wrapped in a dress of humorous expression; sometimes it lurketh under an odd similitude; sometimes it is lodged in a sly question, in a smart answer, in a quirkish reason, in a shrewd intimation, in cunningly diverting, or cleverly retorting an objection: sometimes it is couched in a bold scheme of speech, in a tart irony, in a lusty hyperbole, in a startling metaphor, in a plausible reconciling of contradictions, or in acute nonsense: sometimes a scenical representation of persons or things, a counterfeit speech, a mimical look or gesture passeth for it: sometimes an affected simplicity, sometimes a presumptuous bluntness giveth it being; sometimes it riseth from a lucky hitting upon what is strange, sometimes from a crafty wresting obvious matter to the purpose: often it consisteth in one knows not what, and springeth up one can hardly tell how. Its ways are unaccountable and inexplicable, being answerable to the numberless rovings of fancy and windings of language. It is in short, a manner of speaking out of the simple and plain way (such as reason teacheth and proveth things by), which by a pretty surprising uncouthness in conceit or expression doth affect and amuse the fancy, stirring in it some wonder, and breeding some delight thereto. It raiseth admiration, as signifying a nimble sagacity of apprehension, a special felicity of invention, a vivacity of spirit, and reach of wit more than vulgar: it seeming to argue a rare quickness of parts, that one can fetch in remote conceits applicable; a notable skill, that he can dexterously accommodate them to the purpose before him; together with a lively briskness of humour, not apt to damp those sportful flashes of imagination. (Whence in Aristotle such persons are termed επιδεξιοι, dexterous men; and ευτροποι, men of facile or versatile manners, who can easily turn themselves to all things, or turn all things to themselves.) It also procureth delight, by gratifying curiosity with its rareness or semblance of difficulty (as monsters, not for their beauty, but their rarety; as juggling tricks, not for their use, but their abstruseness, are beheld with pleasure) by diverting the mind from its road of serious thoughts; by instilling gaiety and airiness of spirit; by provoking to such dispositions of spirit in way of emulation or complaisance; and by seasoning matters, otherwise distasteful or insipid, with an unusual, and thence grateful tang.

But saying no more concerning what it is, and leaving it to your imagination and experience to supply the defect of such explication, I shall address myself to show, first, when and how such a manner of speaking may be allowed; then, in what matters and ways it should be condemned.

1. Such facetiousness is not absolutely unreasonable or unlawful, which ministereth harmless divertisement, and delight to conversation (harmless, I say, that is, not entrenching upon piety, not infringing charity or justice, not disturbing peace). For Christianity is not so tetrical, so harsh, so envious, as to bar us continually from innocent, much less from wholesome and useful pleasure, such as human life doth need or require. And if jocular discourse may serve to good purposes of this kind; if it may be apt to raise our drooping

spirits, to allay our irksome cares, to whet our blunted industry, to recreate our minds being tired and cloyed with graver occupations; if it may breed alacrity, or maintain good humour among us; if it may conduce to sweeten conversation and endear society; then is it not inconvenient, or unprofitable. If for those ends we may use other recreations, employing on them our ears and eyes, our hands and feet, our other instruments of sense and motion, why may we not as well to them accommodate our organs of speech and interior sense? Why should those games which excite our wits and fancies be less reasonable than those whereby our grosser parts and faculties are exercised? Yea, why are not those more reasonable, since they are performed in a manly way, and have in them a smack of reason; feeling also they may be so managed, as not only to divert and please, but to improve and profit the mind, rousing and quickening it, yea sometimes enlightening and instructing it, by good sense conveyed in jocular expression?

It would surely be hard that we should be tied ever to knit the brow, and squeeze the brain (to be always sadly dumpish, or seriously pensive), that all divertisement of mirth and pleasantness should be shut out of conversation; and how can we better relieve our minds, or relax our thoughts, how can we be more ingenuously cheerful, in what more kindly way can we exhilarate ourselves and others, than by thus sacrificing to the Graces, as the ancients called it? Are not some persons always, and all persons sometimes, incapable otherwise to divert themselves, than by such discourse? Shall we, I say, have no recreation? or must our recreations be ever clownish, or childish, consisting merely in rustical efforts, or in petty sleights of bodily strength and activity? Were we, in fine, obliged ever to talk like philosophers, assigning dry reasons for everything, and dropping grave sentences upon all occasions, would it not much deaden human life, and make ordinary conversation exceedingly to languish? Facetiousness therefore in such cases, and to such purposes, may be allowable.

2. Facetiousness is allowable when it is the most proper instrument of exposing things apparently base and vile to due contempt. It is many times expedient, that things really ridiculous should appear such, that they may be sufficiently loathed and shunned; and to render them such is the part of a facetious wit, and usually can

only be compassed thereby. When to impugn them with down-right reason, or to check them by serious discourse, would signify nothing, then representing them in a shape strangely ugly to the fancy, and thereby raising derision at them, may effectually discountenance them. Thus did the prophet Elias expose the wicked superstition of those who worshipped Baal: "Elias (saith the text) mocked them, and said, 'Cry aloud; for he is a god, either he is talking, or he is pursuing, or he is in a journey, or peradventure he sleeps, and must be awaked.'" By which one pregnant instance it appeareth that reasoning pleasantly-abusive in some cases may be useful. The Holy Scripture doth not indeed use it frequently (it not suiting the Divine simplicity and stately gravity thereof to do so); yet its condescension thereto at any time sufficiently doth authorise a cautious use thereof. When sarcastic twitches are needful to pierce the thick skins of men, to correct their lethargic stupidity, to rouse them out of their drowsy negligence, then may they well be applied when plain declarations will not enlighten people to discern the truth and weight of things, and blunt arguments will not penetrate to convince or persuade them to their duty, then doth reason freely resign its place to wit, allowing it to undertake its work of instruction and reproof.

3. Facetious discourse particularly may be commodious for reproving some vices, and reclaiming some persons (as salt for cleansing and curing some sores). It commonly procureth a more easy access to the ears of men, and worketh a stronger impression on their hearts, than other discourse could do. Many who will not stand a direct reproof, and cannot abide to be plainly admonished of their fault, will yet endure to be pleasantly rubbed, and will patiently bear a jocund wipe; though they abominate all language purely bitter or sour, yet they can relish discourse having in it a pleasant tartness. You must not chide them as their master, but you may gibe with them as their companion. If you do that, they will take you for pragmatical and haughty; this they may interpret friendship and freedom. Most men are of that temper; and particularly the genius of divers persons, whose opinions and practices we should strive to correct, doth require not a grave and severe, but a free and merry way of treating them. For what can be more unsuitable and unpromising, than to seem serious with those who are not

so themselves, or demure with the scornful? If we design either to please or vex them into better manners, we must be as sportful in a manner, or as contemptuous as themselves. If we mean to be heard by them, we must talk in their own fashion, with humour and jollity; if we will instruct them, we must withal somewhat divert them: we must seem to play with them if we think to convey any sober thoughts into them. They scorn to be formally advised or taught; but they may perhaps be slily laughed and lured into a better mind. If by such complaisance we can inveigle those dottrels to hearken to us, we may induce them to consider farther, and give reason some competent scope, some fair play with them. Good reason may be apparelled in the garb of wit, and therein will securely pass whither in its native homeliness it could never arrive: and being come thither, it with especial advantage may impress good advice, making an offender more clearly to see, and more deeply to feel his miscarriage; being represented to his fancy in a strain somewhat rare and remarkable, yet not so fierce and frightful. The severity of reproof is tempered, and the reprover's anger disguised thereby. The guilty person cannot but observe that he who thus reprehends him is not disturbed or out of humour, and that he rather pitieth than hateth him; which breedeth a veneration to him, and imparteth no small efficacy to his wholesome suggestions. Such a reprehension, while it forceth a smile without, doth work remorse within; while it seemeth to tickle the ear, doth sting the heart. In fine, many whose foreheads are brazed and hearts steeled against all blame, are yet not of proof against derision; divers, who never will be reasoned, may be rallied in better order: in which cases raillery, as an instrument of so important good, as a servant of the best charity, may be allowed.

4. Some errors likewise in this way may be most properly and most successfully confuted; such as deserve not, and hardly can bear a serious and solid confutation. He that will contest things apparently decided by sense and experience, or who disavows clear principles of reason, approved by general consent and the common sense of men, what other hopeful way is there of proceeding with him, than pleasantly to explode his conceits? To dispute seriously with him were trifling; to trifle with him is the proper course. Since he rejecteth the grounds of reasoning, 'tis vain to be in earnest; what then remains but to jest with him? To deal seriously were to yield

too much respect to such a baffler, and too much weight to his fancies; to raise the man too high in his courage and conceit; to make his pretences seem worthy the considering and canvassing. Briefly, perverse obstinacy is more easily quelled, petulant impudence is sooner dashed, sophistical captiousness is more safely eluded, sceptical wantonness is more surely confounded in this than in the simple way of discourse.

5. This way is also commonly the best way of defence against unjust reproach and obloquy. To yield to a slanderous reviler a serious reply, or to make a formal plea against his charge, doth seem to imply that we much consider or deeply resent it; whereas by pleasant reflection on it we signify the matter only deserves contempt, and that we take ourselves unconcerned therein. So easily without care or trouble may the brunts of malice be declined or repelled.

6. This may be allowed in way of counterbalancing and in compliance to the fashion of others. It would be a disadvantage unto truth and virtue if their defenders were barred from the use of this weapon, since it is that especially whereby the patrons of error and vice do maintain and propagate them. They being destitute of good reason, do usually recommend their absurd and pestilent notions by a pleasantness of conceit and expression, bewitching the fancies of shallow hearers, and inveigling heedless persons to a liking of them; and if, for reclaiming such people, the folly of those seducers may in like manner be displayed as ridiculous and odious, why should that advantage be refused? It is wit that wageth the war against reason, against virtue, against religion; wit alone it is that perverteth so many, and so greatly corrupteth the world. It may, therefore, be needful, in our warfare for those dearest concerns, to sort the manner of our fighting with that of our adversaries, and with the same kind of arms to protect goodness, whereby they do assail it. If wit may happily serve under the banner of truth and virtue, we may impress it for that service; and good it were to rescue so worthy a faculty from so vile abuse. It is the right of reason and piety to command that and all other endowments; folly and impiety do only usurp them. Just and fit therefore it is to wrest them out of so bad hands, to revoke them to their right use and duty.

It doth especially seem requisite to do it in this age, wherein plain reason is deemed a dull and heavy thing. When the mental appetite of men is become like the corporal, and cannot relish any food without some piquant sauce, so that people will rather starve than live on solid fare; when substantial and sound discourse findeth small attention or acceptance; in such a time, he that can, may in complaisance, and for fashion's sake, vouchsafe to be facetious; an ingenious vein coupled with an honest mind may be a good talent; he shall employ wit commendably who by it can further the interests of goodness, alluring men first to listen, then inducing them to consent unto its wholesome dictates and precepts.

Since men are so irreclaimably disposed to mirth and laughter, it may be well to set them in the right pin, to divert their humour into the proper channel, that they may please themselves in deriding things which deserve it, ceasing to laugh at that which requireth reverence or horror.

It may also be expedient to put the world out of conceit that all sober and good men are a sort of such lumpish or sour people that they can utter nothing but flat and drowsy stuff, by showing them that such persons, when they see cause, in condescension, can be as brisk and smart as themselves; when they please, can speak pleasantly and wittily, as well as gravely and judiciously. This way at least, in respect to the various palates of men, may for variety sake be sometimes attempted, when other means do fail; when many strict and subtle arguings, many zealous declamations, many wholesome serious discourses have been spent, without effecting the extirpation of bad principles, or conversion of those who abet them; this course may be tried, and some perhaps may be reclaimed thereby.

7. Furthermore, the warrantableness of this practice in some cases may be inferred from a parity of reason, in this manner. If it be lawful (as by the best authorities it plainly doth appear to be), in using rhetorical schemes, poetical strains, involutions of sense in allegories, fables, parables, and riddles, to discoast from the plain and simple way of speech, why may not facetiousness, issuing from the same principles, directed to the same ends, serving to like purposes, be likewise used blamelessly? If those exorbitancies of speech may

be accommodated to instill good doctrine into the head, to excite good passions in the heart, to illustrate and adorn the truth, in a delightful and taking way, and facetious discourse be sometimes notoriously conducible to the same ends, why, they being retained, should it be rejected, especially considering how difficult often it may be to distinguish those forms of discourse from this, or exactly to define the limits which sever rhetoric and raillery. Some elegant figures and trophies of rhetoric (biting sarcasms, sly ironies, strong metaphors, lofty hyperboles, paronomasies, oxymorons, and the like, frequently used by the best speakers, and not seldom even by sacred writers) do lie very near upon the confines of jocularity, and are not easily differenced from those sallies of wit wherein the lepid way doth consist: so that were this wholly culpable, it would be matter of scruple whether one hath committed a fault or no when he meant only to play the orator or the poet; and hard surely it would be to find a judge who could precisely set out the difference between a jest and a flourish.

8. I shall only add, that of old even the sagest and gravest persons (persons of most rigid and severe virtue) did much affect this kind of discourse, and did apply it to noble purposes. The great introducer of moral wisdom among the pagans did practise it so much (by it repressing the windy pride and fallacious vanity of sophisters in his time), that he thereby got the name of ο εἴρων, the droll; and the rest of those who pursued his design do, by numberless stories and apophthegms recorded of them, appear well skilled and much delighted in this way. Many great princes (as Augustus Cfsar, for one, many of whose jests are extant in Macrobius), many grave statesmen (as Cicero particularly, who composed several books of jests), many famous captains (as Fabius, M. Cato the Censor, Scipio Africanus, Epaminondas, Themistocles, Phocion, and many others, whose witty sayings together with their martial exploits are reported by historians), have pleased themselves herein, and made it a condiment of their weighty businesses. So that practising thus (within certain rule and compass), we cannot err without great patterns, and mighty patrons.

9. In fine, since it cannot be shown that such a sportfulness of wit and fancy doth contain an intrinsic and inseparable turpitude; since it may be so cleanly, handsomely, and innocently used, as not to

defile or discompose the mind of the speaker, nor to wrong or harm the hearer, nor to derogate from any worthy subject of discourse, nor to infringe decency, to disturb peace, to violate any of the grand duties incumbent on us (piety, charity, justice, sobriety), but rather sometimes may yield advantage in those respects; it cannot well absolutely and universally be condemned: and when not used upon improper matter, in an unfit manner, with excessive measure, at undue season, to evil purpose, it may be allowed. It is bad objects, or bad adjuncts, which do spoil its indifference and innocence; it is the abuse thereof, to which (as all pleasant things are dangerous, and apt to degenerate into baits of intemperance and excess) it is very liable, that corrupteth it; and seemeth to be the ground why in so general terms it is prohibited by the Apostle. Which prohibition to what cases, or what sorts of jesting it extendeth, we come now to declare.

II. 1. All profane jesting, all speaking loosely and wantonly about holy things (things nearly related to God and religion), making such things the matters of sport and mockery, playing and trifling with them, is certainly prohibited, as an intolerably vain and wicked practice. It is an infallible sign of a vain and light spirit, which considereth little, and cannot distinguish things, to talk slightly concerning persons of high dignity, to whom especial respect is due; or about matters of great importance, which deserve very serious consideration. No man speaketh, or should speak, of his prince, that which he hath not weighed whether it will consist with that veneration which should be preserved inviolate to him. And is not the same, is not much greater care to be used in regard to the incomparably great and glorious Majesty of Heaven? Yes, surely, as we should not without great awe think of Him; so we should not presume to mention His name, His word, His institutions, anything immediately belonging to Him, without profoundest reverence and dread. It is the most enormous sauciness that can be imagined, to speak petulantly or pertly concerning Him; especially considering that whatever we do say about Him, we do utter it in His presence, and to His very face. "For there is not," as the holy psalmist considered, "a word in my tongue, but lo, O Lord, thou knowest it altogether." No man also hath the heart to droll, or thinks raillery convenient, in cases nearly touching his life, his health, his estate, or his fame: and are the true life and health of our soul, are interests in God's favour and mercy, are everlasting glory and bliss affairs of less moment? are the treasures and joys of paradise, or the damages and torments in hell, more jesting matters? No, certainly no: in all reason therefore it becometh us, and it infinitely concerneth us, whenever we think of these things, to be in best earnest, always to speak of them in most sober sadness.

The proper objects of common mirth and sportful divertisement are mean and petty matters; anything at least is by playing therewith made such: great things are thereby diminished and debased; especially sacred things do grievously suffer thence, being with extreme indecency and indignity depressed beneath themselves, when they become the subjects of flashy wit, or the entertainments of frothy merriment: to sacrifice their honour to our vain pleasure, being like the ridiculous fondness of that people which, as Flian reporteth, worshipping a fly, did offer up an ox thereto. These things were by God instituted, and proposed to us for purposes quite different; to compose our hearts, and settle our fancies in a most serious frame; to breed inward satisfaction, and joy purely spiritual; to exercise our most solemn thoughts, and employ our gravest discourses: all our speech therefore about them should be wholesome, apt to afford good instruction, or to excite good affections; "good," as St. Paul speaketh, "for the use of edifying, that it may minister grace unto the hearers."

If we must be facetious and merry, the field is wide and spacious; there are matters enough in the world besides these most august and dreadful things, to try our faculties and please our humour with; everywhere light and ludicrous things occur; it therefore doth argue a marvellous poverty of wit, and barrenness of invention (no less than a strange defect of goodness, and want of discretion), in those who can devise no other subjects to frolic upon besides these, of all most improper and perilous; who cannot seem ingenious under the charge of so highly trespassing upon decency, disclaiming wisdom, wounding the ears of others, and their own consciences. Seem ingenious, I say; for seldom those persons really are such, or are capable to discover any wit in a wise and manly way. 'Tis not the excellency of their fancies, which in themselves are usually sorry and insipid enough, but the uncouthness of their presumption; not their extraordinary wit, but their prodigious rashness, which is to be admired. They are gazed on, as the doers of bold tricks, who dare perform that which no sober man will attempt: they do indeed rather deserve themselves to be laughed at, than their conceits. For what can be more ridiculous than we do make ourselves, when we thus fiddle and fool with our own souls; when, to make vain people merry, we incense God's earnest displeasure; when, to raise a fit of present laughter, we expose ourselves to endless wailing and woe; when, to be reckoned wits, we prove ourselves stark wild? Surely to this case we may accommodate that of a truly great wit, King Solomon: "I said of laughter, It is mad; and of mirth, What doeth it?"

2. All injurious, abusive, scurrilous jesting, which causelessly or needlessly tendeth to the disgrace, damage, vexation, or prejudice in any kind of our neighbour (provoking his displeasure, grating on his modesty, stirring passion in him), is also prohibited. When men, to raise an admiration of their wit, to please themselves, or gratify the humours of other men, do expose their neighbour to scorn and contempt, making ignominious reflections upon his person and his actions, taunting his real imperfections, or fastening imaginary ones upon him, they transgress their duty, and abuse their wits; 'tis not urbanity, or genuine facetiousness, but uncivil rudeness or vile malignity. To do thus, as it is the office of mean and base spirits (unfit for any worthy or weighty employments), so it is full of inhumanity, of iniquity, of indecency and folly. For the weaknesses of men, of what kind soever (natural or moral, in quality or in act), considering whence they spring, and how much we are all subject to them, and do need excuse for them, do in equity challenge compassion to be had of them; not complacency to be taken in them, or mirth drawn from them; they, in respect to common humanity, should rather be studiously connived at, and concealed, or mildly excused, than wilfully laid open, and wantonly descanted upon; they rather are to be deplored secretly, than openly derided.

The reputation of men is too noble a sacrifice to be offered up to vainglory, fond pleasure, or ill-humour; it is a good far more dear and precious, than to be prostituted for idle sport and divertisement. It becometh us not to trifle with that which in common estimation is of so great moment—to play rudely with a thing so very brittle, yet of so vast price; which being once broken or cracked, it is very hard and scarce possible to repair. A small, transient pleasure, a tickling the ears, wagging the lungs, forming the face into a smile, a giggle, or a hum, are not to be purchased with the grievous distaste and smart, perhaps with the real damage and mischief of our neighbour, which attend upon contempt. This is not jesting, surely, but bad earnest; 'tis wild mirth, which is the mother of grief to those whom we should tenderly love; 'tis unnatural sport, which breedeth displeasure in them whose delight it should promote, whose liking it should procure: it crosseth the nature and design of this way of speaking, which is to cement and ingratiate society, to render conversation pleasant and sprightly, for mutual satisfaction and comfort.

True festivity is called salt, and such it should be, giving a smart but savoury relish to discourse; exciting an appetite, not irritating disgust; cleansing sometimes, but never creating a sore: and εαν μωρανθη, (if it become thus insipid), or unsavoury, it is therefore good for nothing, but to be cast out, and trodden under foot of men. Such jesting which doth not season wholesome or harmless discourse, but giveth a *haut goŝt* to putrid and poisonous stuff, gratifying distempered palates and corrupt stomachs, is indeed odious and despicable folly, to be cast out with loathing, to be trodden under foot with contempt. If a man offends in this sort, to please himself, 'tis scurvy malignity; if to delight others, 'tis base servility and flattery: upon the first score he is a buffoon to himself; upon the last, a fool to others. And well in common speech are such practisers so termed, the grounds of that practice being so vain, and the effect so unhappy. The heart of fools, saith the wise man, is in the house of mirth; meaning, it seems, especially such hurtfully wanton mirth: for it is (as he further telleth us) the property of fools to delight in doing harm ("It is as sport to a fool to do mischief"). Is it not in earnest most palpable folly, for so mean ends to do so great harm; to disoblige men in sport; to lose friends and get enemies for a conceit; out of a light humour to provoke fierce wrath, and breed tough hatred; to engage one's self consequently very far in strife, danger, and trouble? No way certainly is more apt to produce such effects than this; nothing more speedily inflameth, or more thoroughly engageth men, or sticketh longer in men's hearts and memories, than bitter taunts and scoffs: whence this honey soon turns into gall; these jolly comedies do commonly terminate in woeful tragedies.

Especially this scurrilous and scoffing way is then most detestable when it not only exposeth the blemishes and infirmities of men, but abuseth piety and virtue themselves; flouting persons for their constancy in devotion, or their strict adherence to a conscientious practice of duty; aiming to effect that which Job complaineth of, "The just upright man is laughed to scorn;" resembling those whom the psalmist thus describeth, "Who whet their tongue like a sword, and bend their arrows, even bitter words, that they may shoot in secret at the perfect;" serving good men as Jeremy was served—"The word of the Lord," saith he, "was made a reproach unto me, and a derision daily."

This practice doth evidently in the highest degree tend to the disparagement and discouragement of goodness; aiming to expose it, and to render men ashamed thereof; and it manifestly proceedeth from a desperate corruption of mind, from a mind hardened and emboldened, sold and enslaved to wickedness: whence they who deal therein are in Holy Scripture represented as egregious sinners, or persons superlatively wicked, under the name of scorners (Λοιμους, pests, or pestilent men, the Greek translators call them, properly enough in regard to the effects of their practice); concerning whom the wise man (signifying how God will meet with them in their own way) saith, "Surely the Lord scorneth the scorners." Ἐμπαικτας (scoffers, or mockers), St. Peter termeth them, who walk according to their own lusts; who not being willing to practise, are ready to deride virtue; thereby striving to seduce others into their pernicious courses.

This offence also proportionably groweth more criminal as it presumeth to reach persons eminent in dignity or worth, unto whom special veneration is appropriate. This adjoineth sauciness to scurrility, and advanceth the wrong thereof into a kind of sacrilege. 'Tis not only injustice, but profaneness, to abuse the gods. Their station is a sanctuary from all irreverence and reproach; they are seated on high, that we may only look up to them with respect; their defects are not to be seen, or not to be touched by malicious or wanton wits, by spiteful or scornful tongues: the diminution of their credit is a public mischief, and the State itself doth suffer in their becoming objects of scorn; not only themselves are vilified and degraded, but the great affairs they manage are obstructed, the justice they administer is disparaged thereby.

In fine, no jesting is allowable which is not thoroughly innocent: it is an unworthy perverting of wit to employ it in biting and scratching; in working prejudice to any man's reputation or interest; in needlessly incensing any man's anger or sorrow; in raising animosities, dissensions, and feuds among any.

Whence it is somewhat strange that any men from so mean and silly a practice should expect commendation, or that any should afford regard thereto; the which it is so far from meriting, that indeed contempt and abhorrence are due to it. Men do truly more render themselves despicable than others when, without just ground, or reasonable occasion, they do attack others in this way. That such a practice doth ever find any encouragement or acceptance, whence can it proceed, but from the bad nature and small judgment of some persons? For to any man who is endowed with any sense of goodness, and hath a competence of true wit, or a right knowledge of good manners (who knows. . . . *inurbanum lepido seponere dicto*), it cannot but be unsavoury and loathsome. The repute it obtaineth is in all respects unjust. So would it appear, not only were the cause to be decided in a court of morality, because it consists not with virtue and wisdom; but even before any competent judges of wit itself. For he overthrows his own pretence, and cannot reasonably claim any interest in wit, who doth thus behave himself: he prejudgeth himself to want wit, who cannot descry fit matter to divert himself or others: he discovereth a great straitness and sterility of good invention, who cannot in all the wide field of things find better subjects of discourse; who knows not how to be ingenious within reasonable compass, but to pick up a sorry conceit is forced to make excursions beyond the bounds of honesty and decency.

Neither is it any argument of considerable ability in him that haps to please this way: a slender faculty will serve the turn. The sharpness of his speech cometh not from wit so much as from choler, which furnisheth the lowest inventions with a kind of pungent expression, and giveth an edge to every spiteful word: so that any dull wretch doth seem to scold eloquently and ingeniously. Commonly also satirical taunts do owe their seeming piquancy, not to the speaker or his words, but to the subject, and the hearers; the matter conspiring with the bad nature or the vanity of men who love to laugh at any rate, and to be pleased at the expense of other men's repute; conceiting themselves extolled by the depression of their neighbour, and hoping to gain by his loss. Such customers they are that maintain the bitter wits, who otherwise would want trade, and might go a-begging. For commonly they who seem to excel this way are miserably flat in other discourse, and most dully serious: they have a particular unaptness to describe any good thing, or commend any worthy person; being destitute of right ideas, and proper terms answerable to such purposes: their representations of that kind are absurd and unhandsome; their eulogies (to use their own way of speaking) are in effect satires, and they can hardly more abuse a man than by attempting to commend him; like those in the prophet, who were wise to do ill, but to do well had no knowledge.

3. I pass by that it is very culpable to be facetious in obscene and smutty matters. Such things are not to be discoursed on either in jest or in earnest; they must not, as St. Paul saith, be so much as named among Christians. To meddle with them is not to disport, but to defile one's self and others. There is indeed no more certain sign of a mind utterly debauched from piety and virtue than by affecting such talk. But further—

4. All unseasonable jesting is blamable. As there are some proper seasons of relaxation, when we may *desipere in loco*; so there are some times, and circumstances of things, wherein it concerneth and becometh men to be serious in mind, grave in demeanour, and plain in discourse; when to sport in this way is to do indecently or uncivilly, to be impertinent or troublesome.

It comporteth not well with the presence of superiors, before whom it becometh us to be composed and modest, much less with the performance of sacred offices, which require an earnest attention, and most serious frame of mind.

In deliberations and debates about affairs of great importance, the simple manner of speaking to the point is the proper, easy, clear, and compendious way: facetious speech there serves only to obstruct and entangle business, to lose time, and protract the result. The shop and exchange will scarce endure jesting in their lower transactions: the Senate, the Court of Justice, the Church do much more exclude it from their more weighty consultations. Whenever it justleth out, or hindereth the despatch of other serious business, taking up the room or swallowing the time due to it, or indisposing the minds of the audience to attend it, then it is unseasonable and pestilent. Παιζειν ινα σπουδαζης (to play, that we may be seriously busy), is the good rule (of Anacharsis), implying the subordination of sport to business, as a condiment and furtherance, not an impediment or clog thereto. He that for his sport neglects his business, deserves indeed to be reckoned among children; and children's fortune will attend him, to be pleased with toys, and to fail of substantial profit.

'Tis again improper (because indeed uncivil, and inhuman) to jest with persons that are in a sad or afflicted condition; as arguing want of due considering or due commiserating their case. It appears a kind of insulting upon their misfortune, and is apt to foment their grief. Even in our own case (upon any disastrous occurrence to ourselves), it would not be seemly to frolic it thus; it would signify want of due regard to the frowns of God, and the strokes of His hand; it would cross the wise man's advice, "In the day of prosperity be joyful, but in the day of adversity consider."

It is also not seasonable, or civil, to be jocund in this way with those who desire to be serious, and like not the humour. Jocularity should not be forcibly obtruded, but by a kindly conspiracy (or tacit compact) slip into conversation; consent and complaisance give all the life thereto. Its design is to sweeten and ease society; when to the contrary it breedeth offence or encumbrance, it is worse than vain and unprofitable. From these instances we may collect when in other like cases it is unseasonable, and therefore culpable. Further—

5. To affect, admire, or highly to value this way of speaking (either absolutely in itself, or in comparison to the serious and plain way of speech), and thence to be drawn into an immoderate use thereof, is blamable. A man of ripe age and sound judgment, for refreshment to himself, or in complaisance to others, may some-

times condescend to play in this, or any other harmless way; but to be fond of it, to prosecute it with a careful or painful eagerness, to dote and dwell upon it, to reckon it a brave or a fine thing, a singular matter of commendation, a transcendent accomplishment, anywise preferable to rational endowments, or comparable to the moral excellencies of our mind (to solid knowledge, or sound wisdom, or true virtue and goodness), this is extremely childish, or brutish, and far below a man. What can be more absurd than to make business of play, to be studious and laborious in toys, to make a profession or drive a trade of impertinency? What more plain nonsense can there be, than to be earnest in jest, to be continual in divertisement, or constant in pastime; to make extravagance all our way, and sauce all our diet? Is not this plainly the life of a child that is ever busy, yet never hath anything to do? Or the life of that mimical brute which is always active in playing uncouth and unlucky tricks; which, could it speak, might surely pass well for a professed wit?

The proper work of man, the grand drift of human life, is to follow reason (that noble spark kindled from Heaven; that princely and powerful faculty, which is able to reach so lofty objects, and achieve so mighty works), not to soothe fancy, that brutish, shallow and giddy power, able to perform nothing worthy much regard. We are not (even Cicero could tell us) born for play and jesting, but for severity, and the study of graver and greater affairs. Yes, we were purposely designed, and fitly framed, to understand and contemplate, to affect and delight in, to undertake and pursue most noble and worthy things; to be employed in business considerably profitable to ourselves, and beneficial to others. We do therefore strangely debase ourselves, when we do strongly bend our minds to, or set our affections upon, such toys.

Especially to do so is unworthy of a Christian; that is, of a person who is advanced to so high a rank, and so glorious relations; who hath so excellent objects of his mind and affections presented before him, and so excellent rewards for his care and pains proposed to him; who is engaged in affairs of so worthy nature, and so immense consequence: for him to be zealous about quibbles, for him to be ravished with puny conceits and expressions, 'tis a wondrous oversight, and an enormous indecency.

He indeed that prefers any faculty to reason, disclaims the privilege of being a man, and understands not the worth of his own nature; he that prizes any quality beyond virtue and goodness, renounces the title of a Christian, and knows not how to value the dignity of his profession. It is these two (reason and virtue) in conjunction which produce all that is considerably good and great in the world. Fancy can do little; doth never anything well, except as directed and wielded by them. Do pretty conceits or humorous talk carry on any business, or perform any work? No; they are ineffectual and fruitless: often they disturb, but they never despatch anything with good success. It is simple reason (as dull and dry as it seemeth) which expediteth all the grand affairs, which accomplisheth all the mighty works that we see done in the world. In truth, therefore, as one diamond is worth numberless bits of glass; so one solid reason is worth innumerable fancies: one grain of true science and sound wisdom in real worth and use doth outweigh loads (if any loads can be) of freakish wit. To rate things otherwise doth argue great weakness of judgment, and fondness of mind. So to conceit of this way signifieth a weak mind; and much to delight therein rendereth it so—nothing more debaseth the spirit of a man, or more rendereth it light and trifling.

Hence if we must be venting pleasant conceits, we should do it as if we did it not, carelessly and unconcernedly; not standing upon it, or valuing ourselves for it: we should do it with measure and moderation; not giving up ourselves thereto, so as to mind it or delight in it more than in any other thing: we should not be so intent upon it as to become remiss in affairs more proper or needful for us; so as to nauseate serious business, or disrelish the more worthy entertainments of our minds. This is the great danger of it, which we daily see men to incur; they are so bewitched with a humour of being witty themselves, or of hearkening to the fancies of others, that it is this only which they can like or favour, which they can endure to think or talk of. 'Tis a great pity that men who would seem to have so much wit, should so little understand themselves. But further—

6. Vainglorious ostentation this way is very blamable. All ambition, all vanity, all conceitedness, upon whatever ground they are founded, are absolutely unreasonable and silly; but yet those being

grounded on some real ability, or some useful skill, are wise and manly in comparison to this, which standeth on a foundation so manifestly slight and weak. The old philosophers by a severe father were called *animalia glorif* (animals of glory), and by a satirical poet they were termed bladders of vanity; but they at least did catch at praise from praiseworthy knowledge; they were puffed up with a wind which blew some good to mankind; they sought glory from that which deserved glory if they had not sought it; it was a substantial and solid credit which they did affect, resulting from successful enterprises of strong reason, and stout industry: but these *animalculf glorif*, these flies, these insects of glory, these, not bladders, but bubbles of vanity, would be admired and praised for that which is nowise admirable or laudable; for the casual hits and emergencies of roving fancy; for stumbling on an odd conceit or phrase, which signifieth nothing, and is as superficial as the smile, as hollow as the noise it causeth. Nothing certainly in nature is more ridiculous than a self-conceited wit, who deemeth himself somebody, and greatly pretendeth to commendation from so pitiful and worthless a thing as a knack of trifling.

7. Lastly, it is our duty never so far to engage ourselves in this way as thereby to lose or to impair that habitual seriousness, modesty and sobriety of mind, that steady composedness, gravity and constancy of demeanour, which become Christians. We should continually keep our minds intent upon our high calling, and grand interests; ever well tuned, and ready for the performance of holy devotions, and the practice of most serious duties with earnest attention and fervent affection. Wherefore we should never suffer them to be dissolved into levity, or disordered into a wanton frame, indisposing us for religious thoughts and actions. We ought always in our behaviour to maintain, not only το πρεπον (a fitting decency), but also το σεμνον (a stately gravity), a kind of venerable majesty, suitable to that high rank which we bear of God's friends and children; adorning our holy profession, and guarding us from all impressions of sinful vanity. Wherefore we should not let ourselves be transported into any excessive pitch of lightness, inconsistent with or prejudicial to our Christian state and business. Gravity and modesty are the senses of piety, which being once slighted, sin will easily attempt and encroach upon us. So the old Spanish gentleman

may be interpreted to have been wise who, when his son upon a voyage to the Indies took his leave of him, gave him this odd advice, "My son, in the first place keep thy gravity, in the next place fear God;" intimating that a man must first be serious, before he can be pious.

To conclude, as we need not be demure, so must we not be impudent; as we should not be sour, so ought we not to be fond; as we may be free, so we should not be vain; as we may well stoop to friendly complaisance, so we should take heed of falling into contemptible levity. If without wronging others, or derogating from ourselves, we can be facetious, if we can use our wits in jesting innocently, and conveniently, we may sometimes do it: but let us, in compliance with St. Paul's direction, beware of "foolish talking and jesting which are not convenient."

"Now the God of grace and peace . . . . make us perfect in every good work to do His will, working in us that which is well pleasing in His sight, through Jesus Christ, to whom be glory for ever and ever. Amen."

AGAINST RASH AND VAIN SWEARING.

"But above all things, my brethren, swear not."
St. James v. 12.

Among other precepts of good life (directing the practice of virtue and abstinence from sin) St. James doth insert this about swearing, couched in expression denoting his great earnestness, and apt to excite our special attention. Therein he doth not mean universally to interdict the use of oaths, for that in some cases is not only lawful, but very expedient, yea, needful, and required from us as a duty; but that swearing which our Lord had expressly prohibited to His disciples, and which thence, questionless, the brethren to whom St. James did write did well understand themselves obliged to forbear, having learned so in the first catechisms of Christian institution; that is, needless and heedless swearing in ordinary conversation, a practice then frequent in the world, both among Jews and Gentiles; the which also, to the shame of our age, is now so much in fashion, and with some men in vogue; the invoking God's name, appealing to His testimony, and provoking His judgment upon any slight occasion, in common talk, with vain incogitancy, or profane boldness. From such practice the Holy Apostle exhorteth in terms importing his great concernedness, and implying the matter to be of highest importance; for, Προ παντων, saith he, "(Before all things), my brethren, do not swear;" as if he did apprehend this sin of all others to be one of the most heinous and pernicious. Could he have said more? would he have said so much, if he had not conceived the matter to be of exceeding weight and consequence? And that it is so, I mean now, by God's help, to show you, by proposing some considerations, whereby the heinous wickedness, together with the monstrous folly, of such rash and vain swearing will appear; the which being laid to heart will, I hope, effectually dissuade and deter from it.

I. Let us consider the nature of an oath, and what we do when we adventure to swear.

It is (as it is phrased in the Decalogue, and elsewhere in Holy Scripture) an assuming the name of God, and applying it to our purpose; to countenance and confirm what we say.

It is an invocation of God as a most faithful Witness, concerning the truth of our words, or the sincerity of our meaning.

It is an appeal to God as a most upright Judge whether we do prevaricate in asserting what we do not believe true, or in promising what we are not firmly resolved to perform.

It is a formal engagement of God to be the Avenger of our trespassing in violation of truth or faith.

It is a binding our souls with a most strict and solemn obligation, to answer before God, and to undergo the issue of His judgment about what we affirm or undertake.

Such an oath is represented to us in Holy Scripture.

Whence we may collect, that swearing doth require great modesty and composedness of spirit, very serious consideration and solicitous care, that we be not rude and saucy with God, in taking up His name, and prostituting it to vile or mean uses; that we do not abuse or debase His authority, by citing it to aver falsehoods or impertinences; that we do not slight His venerable justice, by rashly provoking it against us; that we do not precipitately throw our souls into most dangerous snares and intricacies.

For let us reflect and consider: What a presumption is it without due regard and reverence to lay hold on God's name; with unhallowed breath to vent and toss that great and glorious, that most holy, that reverend, that fearful and terrible name of the Lord our God, the great Creator, the mighty Sovereign, the dreadful Judge of all the world; that name which all heaven with profoundest submission doth adore, which the angelical powers, the brightest and purest Seraphim, without hiding their faces, and reverential horror, cannot utter or hear; the very thought whereof should strike awe through our hearts, the mention whereof would make any sober man to tremble? Πως γαρ ουκ ατοπον, "For how," saith St. Chrysostom, "is it not absurd that a servant should not dare to call his master by name, or bluntly and ordinarily to mention him, yet that we slightly and contemptuously should in our mouth toss about the Lord of angels?

"How is it not absurd, if we have a garment better than the rest, that we forbear to use it continually, but in the most slight and common way do wear the name of God?"

How grievous indecency is it, at every turn to summon our Maker, and call down Almighty God from heaven, to attend our leisure, to vouch our idle prattle, to second our giddy passions, to concern His truth, His justice, His power in our trivial affairs!

What a wildness is it, to dally with that judgment upon which the eternal doom of all creatures dependeth, at which the pillars of heaven are astonished, which hurled down legions of angels from the top of heaven and happiness into the bottomless dungeon: the which, as grievous sinners, of all things we have most reason to dread; and about which no sober man can otherwise think than did that great king, the holy psalmist, who said, "My flesh trembleth for Thee, and I am afraid of Thy judgments!"

How prodigious a madness is it, without any constraint or needful cause, to incur so horrible a danger, to rush upon a curse; to defy that vengeance, the least touch of breath whereof can dash us to nothing, or thrust us down into extreme and endless woe?

Who can express the wretchedness of that folly, which so entangleth us with inextricable knots, and enchaineth our souls so rashly with desperate obligations?

Wherefore he that would but a little mind what he doeth when he dareth to swear, what it is to meddle with the adorable name, the venerable testimony, the formidable judgment, the terrible vengeance of the Divine Majesty, into what a case he putteth himself, how extreme hazard he runneth thereby, would assuredly have little heart to swear, without greatest reason, and most urgent need; hardly without trembling would he undertake the most necessary and solemn oath; much cause would he see σεβεσθαι ορκον, to adore, to fear an oath: which to do, the divine preacher maketh the character of a good man. "As," saith he, "is the good, so is the sinner; and he that sweareth, as he that feareth an oath."

In fine, even a heathen philosopher, considering the nature of an oath, did conclude the unlawfulness thereof in such cases. For, "seeing," saith he, "an oath doth call God for witness, and proposeth Him for umpire and voucher of the things it saith; therefore to induce God so upon occasion of human affairs, or, which is all one, upon small and slight accounts, doth imply contempt of Him: wherefore we ought wholly to shun swearing, except upon occasions of highest necessity."

II. We may consider that swearing, agreeably to its nature, or natural aptitude and tendency, is represented in Holy Scripture as a special part of religious worship, or devotion towards God; in the due performance whereof we do avow Him for the true God and Governor of the world; we piously do acknowledge His principal attributes and special prerogatives; His omnipresence and omniscience, extending itself to our most inward thoughts, our secretest purposes, our closest retirements; His watchful providence over all our actions, affairs, and concerns; His faithful goodness, in favouring truth and protecting right; His exact justice, in patronising sincerity, and chastising perfidiousness; His being Supreme Lord over all persons, and Judge paramount in all causes; His readiness in our need, upon our humble imploration and reference, to undertake the arbitration of matters controverted, and the care of administering justice, for the maintenance of truth and right, of loyalty and fidelity, of order and peace among men. Swearing does also intimate a pious truth and confidence in God, as Aristotle observeth.

Such things a serious oath doth imply, to such purposes swearing naturally serveth; and therefore to signify or effectuate them, Divine institution hath devoted it.

God in goodness to such ends hath pleased to lend us His great name; allowing us to cite Him for a witness, to have recourse to His bar, to engage His justice and power, whenever the case deserveth and requireth it, or when we cannot by other means well assure the sincerity of our meaning, or secure the constancy of our resolutions.

Yea, in such exigencies He doth exact this practice from us, as an instance of our religious confidence in Him, and as a service conducible to His glory. For it is a precept in His law, of moral nature, and eternal obligation, "Thou shalt fear the Lord thy God; Him shalt thou serve, and to Him shalt thou cleave, and shalt swear by His name." It is the character of a religious man to swear with due reverence and upright conscience. For, "The king," saith the psalmist, "shall rejoice in God; every one that sweareth by Him shall glory: but the mouth of them that speak lies shall be stopped." It is a distinctive mark of God's people, according to that of the prophet Jeremy, "And it shall come to pass, if they will diligently learn the ways of my people, to swear by my name . . . then shall they be built in the midst of my people." It is predicted concerning the evangelical times, "Unto Me every knee shall bow, every tongue shall swear:" and, "That he who blesseth himself in the earth, shall bless himself by the God of Truth; and he that sweareth in the earth, shall swear by the God of Truth."

As therefore all other acts of devotion, wherein immediate application is made to the Divine Majesty, should never be performed without most hearty intention, most serious consideration, most lowly reverence; so neither should this grand one, wherein God is so nearly touched, and His chief attributes so much concerned: the which indeed doth involve both prayer and praise, doth require the most devotional acts of faith and fear.

We therefore should so perform it as not to incur that reproof: "This people draweth nigh unto me with their mouth, and honoureth me with their lips, but their heart is far from me."

When we seem most formally to avow God, to confess His omniscience, to confide in His justice, we should not really disregard Him, and in effect signify that we do not think He doth know what we say, or what we do.

If we do presume to offer this service, we should do it in the manner appointed by himself, according to the conditions prescribed in the prophet, "Thou shalt swear, the Lord liveth, in truth, in judgment, and in righteousness:" in truth, taking heed that our meaning be conformable to the sense of our words, and our words to the verity of things; in judgment, having with careful deliberation examined and weighed that which we assert or promise; in righteousness, being satisfied in conscience that we do not therein infringe any rule of piety toward God, of equity toward men, or sobriety and discretion in regard to ourselves.

The cause of our swearing must be needful, or very expedient; the design of it must be honest and useful to considerable purposes (tending to God's honour, our neighbour's benefit, our own welfare); the matter of it should be not only just and lawful, but worthy and weighty; the manner ought to be grave and solemn, our mind being framed to earnest attention, and endued with pious affections suitable to the occasion.

Otherwise, if we do venture to swear, without due advice and care, without much respect and awe, upon any slight or vain (not to say bad or unlawful) occasion, we then desecrate swearing, and are guilty of profaning a most sacred ordinance: the doing so doth imply base hypocrisy, or lewd mockery, or abominable wantonness and folly; in bodily invading and vainly trifling with the most august duties of religion. Such swearing therefore is very dishonourable and injurious to God, very prejudicial to religion, very repugnant to piety.

III. We may consider that the swearing prohibited is very noxious to human society.

The great prop of society (which upholdeth the safety, peace, and welfare thereof, in observing laws, dispensing justice, discharging trusts, keeping contracts, and holding good correspondence mutually) is conscience, or a sense of duty toward God, obliging to perform that which is right and equal; quickened by hope of rewards and fear of punishments from Him: secluding which principle, no worldly confederation is strong enough to hold men fast, or can further dispose many to do right, or observe faith, or hold peace, than appetite or interest, or humour (things very slippery and uncertain) do sway them.

That men should live honestly, quietly, and comfortably together, it is needful that they should live under a sense of God's will, and in awe of the divine power, hoping to please God, and fearing to offend Him, by their behaviour respectively.

That justice should be administered between men, it is necessary that testimonies of fact be alleged; and that witnesses should apprehend themselves greatly obliged to discover the truth, according to their conscience, in dark and doubtful cases.

That men should uprightly discharge offices serviceable to public good, it doth behove that they be firmly engaged to perform the trusts reposed in them.

That in affairs of very considerable importance men should deal with one another with satisfaction of mind, and mutual confidence, they must receive competent assurances concerning the integrity, fidelity, and constancy each of other.

That the safety of governors may be preserved, and the obedience due to them maintained secure from attempts to which they are liable (by the treachery, levity, perverseness, timorousness, ambition, all such lusts and ill humours of men), it is expedient that men should be tied with the strictest bands of allegiance.

That controversies emergent about the interests of men should be determined, and an end put to strife by peremptory and satisfactory means, is plainly necessary for common quiet.

Wherefore for the public interest and benefit of human society it is requisite that the highest obligations possible should be laid upon the consciences of men.

And such are those of oaths, engaging them to fidelity and constancy in all such cases, out of regard to Almighty God, as the infallible patron of truth and right, the unavoidable chastiser of perfidiousness and improbity.

To such purposes, therefore, oaths have ever been applied, as the most effectual instruments of working them; not only among the followers of true and perfect religion, but even among all those who had any glimmering notions concerning a Divine Power and Providence; who have deemed an oath the fastest tie of conscience, and held the violation of it for the most detestable impiety and iniquity. So that what Cicero saith of the Romans, that "their ancestors had no band to constrain faith more strait than an oath," is true of all other nations, common reason not being able to devise any engagement more obliging than it is; it being in the nature of things τελευταια πιστις, and ουρωτατον αληθειας ενευρον, the utmost assurance, the last resort of human faith, the surest pledge that any man can yield of his trustiness. Hence ever in transactions of highest moment this hath been used to bind the faith of men.

Hereby nations have been wont to ratify leagues of peace and amity between each other (which therefore the Greeks call οοκια).

Hereby princes have obliged their subjects to loyalty: and it hath ever been the strongest argument to press that duty, which the Preacher useth, "I counsel thee to keep the king's commandment, and that in regard of the oath of God."

Hereby generals have engaged their soldiers to stick close to them in bearing hardships and encountering dangers.

Hereby the nuptial league hath been confirmed; the solemnisation whereof in temples before God is in effect a most sacred oath.

Hereon the decision of the greatest causes concerning the lives, estates, and reputations of men have depended; so that, as the Apostle saith, "an oath for confirmation is to them an end of all strife."

Indeed, such hath the need hereof been ever apprehended, that we may observe, in cases of great importance, no other obligation hath been admitted for sufficient to bind the fidelity and constancy of the most credible persons; so that even the best men hardly could trust the best men without it. For instance,

When Abimelech would assure to himself the friendship of Abraham, although he knew him to be a very pious and righteous person, whose word might be as well taken as any man's, yet, for entire satisfaction, he thus spake to him: "God is with thee in all that thou doest: Now therefore swear unto me here by God, that thou wilt not deal falsely with me."

Abraham, though he did much confide in the honesty of his servant Eliezer, having entrusted him with all his estate, yet in the affair concerning the marriage of his son he could not but thus oblige him: "Put," saith he, "I pray thee, thy hand under my thigh, and I will make thee swear by the Lord, the God of heaven and the God of the earth, that thou wilt not take a wife unto my son of the daughters of the Canaanites."

Laban had good experience of Jacob's fidelity; yet that would not satisfy, but, "The Lord," said he, "watch between me and thee, when we are absent one from another. If thou shalt afflict my daughters, or if thou shalt take other wives beside my daughters, no man is with us; see, God is witness between thee and me. The God of Abraham, and the God of Nahor, the God of their father, judge betwixt us."

So did Jacob make Joseph swear that he would bury him in Canaan: and Joseph caused the children of Israel to swear that they would translate his bones. So did Jonathan cause his beloved friend David to swear that he would show kindness to him and to his house for ever. The prudence of which course the event showeth, the total excision of Jonathan's family being thereby prevented; for "the king," 'tis said, "spared Mephibosheth the son of Jonathan, because of the Lord's oath that was between them."

These instances declare that there is no security which men can yield comparable to that of an oath; the obligation whereof no man wilfully can infringe without renouncing the fear of God and any pretence to His favour.

Wherefore human society will be extremely wronged and damnified by the dissolving or slackening these most sacred bands of conscience; and consequently by their common and careless use, which soon will breed a contempt of them, and render them insignificant, either to bind the swearers, or to ground a trust on their oaths.

As by the rare and reverent use of oaths their dignity is upheld and their obligation kept fast, so by the frequent and negligent application of them, by the prostituting them to every mean and toyish purpose, their respect will be quite lost, their strength will be loosed, they will prove unserviceable to public use.

If oaths generally become cheap and vile, what will that of allegiance signify? If men are wont to play with swearing anywhere, can we expect they should be serious and strict therein at the bar or in the church. Will they regard God's testimony, or dread His judgment, in one place, or at one time, when everywhere upon any, upon no occasion they dare to confront and contemn them? Who then will be the more trusted for swearing? What satisfaction will any man have from it? The rifeness of this practice, as it is the sign, so it will be the cause of a general diffidence among man.

Incredible therefore is the mischief which this vain practice will bring in to the public; depriving princes of their best security, exposing the estates of private men to uncertainty, shaking all the confidence men can have in the faith of one another.

For which detriments accruing from this abuse to the public every vain swearer is responsible; and he would do well to consider that he will never be able to make reparation for them. And the public is much concerned that this enormity be retrenched.

IV. Let us consider, that rash and vain swearing is very apt often to bring the practiser of it into that most horrible sin of perjury. For "false swearing," as the Hebrew wise man saith, "naturally springeth out of much swearing:" and, "he," saith St. Chrysostom, "that sweareth continually, both willingly and unwillingly, both ignorantly and knowingly, both in earnest and in sport, being often transported by anger and many other things, will frequently forswear. It is confessed and manifest, that it is necessary for him that sweareth much to be perjurious." Ἀμηανον γαρ, αμηανον, "For," saith he again, "it is impossible, it is impossible for a mouth addicted to swearing not frequently to forswear." He that sweareth at random, as blind passion moveth, or wanton fancy prompteth, or the temper suggesteth, often will hit upon asserting that which is false, or promising that which is impossible: that want of conscience and of consideration which do suffer him to violate God's law in swearing will betray him to the venting of lies, which backed with oaths become perjuries. If sometime what he sweareth doth happen to be true and performable, it doth not free him of guilt; it being his fortune, rather than his care or conscience, which keepeth him from perjury.

V. Such swearing commonly will induce a man to bind himself by oath to unlawful practices; and consequently will entangle him in a woeful necessity either of breaking his oath, or of doing worse, and committing wickedness: so that "swearing," as St. Chrysostom saith, "hath this misery attending it, that, both trangressed and observed, it plagueth those who are guilty of it."

Of this perplexity the Holy Scripture affordeth two notable instances: the one of Saul, forced to break his rash oaths; the other of Herod, being engaged thereby to commit a most horrid murder.

Had Saul observed his oaths, what injury had he done, what mischief had he produced, in slaughtering his most worthy and most innocent son, the prop and glory of his family, the bulwark of his country, and the grand instrument of salvation to it; in forcing the people to violate their cross oath, and for prevention of one, causing many perjuries? He was therefore fain to desist, and lie under the guilt of breaking his oaths.

And for Herod, the excellent father thus presseth the consideration of his case: "Take," saith he, "I beseech you, the chopped off head of St. John, and his warm blood yet trickling down; each of you bear it home with you, and conceive that before your eyes you hear it uttering speech, and saying, Embrace the murderer of me, an oath. That which reproof did not, this an oath did do; that which the tyrant's wrath could not, this the necessity of keeping an oath did effect. For when the tyrant was reprehended publicly in the audience of all men, he bravely did bear the rebuke; but when he had cast himself into the necessity of oaths, then did he cut off that blessed head."

VI. Likewise the use of rash swearing will often engage a man in undertakings very inconvenient and detrimental to himself. A man is bound to perform his vows to the Lord, whatever they be, whatever damage or trouble thence may accrue to him, if they be not unlawful. It is the law, that which is gone out of thy lips, thou shalt keep and perform. It is the property of a good man, that he sweareth to his own hurt, and changeth not. Wherefore 'tis the part of a sober man to be well advised what he doth swear or vow religiously, that he do not put himself into the inextricable strait of committing great sin, or undergoing great inconvenience; that he do not rush into that snare of which the wise man speaketh, "It is a snare to a man to devour that which is holy (or, to swallow a sacred obligation), and after vows to make inquiry," seeking how he may disengage himself the doing which is a folly offensive to God, as the Preacher telleth us. "When," saith he, "thou vowest a vow unto God, defer not to pay it; for He hath no pleasure in fools: pay that which thou hast vowed." God will not admit our folly in vowing as a plea for non-performance; He will exact it from us both as a due debt, and as a proper punishment of our impious folly.

For instance, into what loss and mischief, what sorrow, what regret and repentance, did the unadvised vow of Jephthah throw him; the performance whereof, as St. Chrysostom remarketh, God did permit, and order to be commemorated with solemn lamentation, that all posterity might be admonished thereby, and deterred from such precipitant swearing.

VII. Let us consider that swearing is a sin of all others peculiarly clamorous, and provocative of Divine judgment. God is hardly so much concerned, or in a manner constrained, to punish any other sin as this. He is bound in honour and interest to vindicate His name from the abuse, His authority from the contempt, His holy ordinance from the profanation, which it doth infer. He is concerned to take care that His providence be not questioned, that the dread of His majesty be not voided, that all religion be not overthrown by the outrageous commission thereof with impunity.

It immediately toucheth His name, it expressly calleth upon Him to mind it, to judge it, to show himself in avenging it. He may seem deaf, or unconcerned, if, being so called and provoked, He doth not declare Himself.

There is understood to be a kind of formal compact between Him and mankind, obliging Him to interpose, to take the matter into His cognisance, being specially addressed to Him.

The bold swearer doth importune Him to hear, doth rouse Him to mark, doth brave Him to judge and punish his wickedness.

Hence no wonder that "the flying roll," a quick and inevitable curse, doth surprise the swearer, and cut him off, as it is in the prophet. No wonder that so many remarkable instances do occur in history of signal vengeance inflicted on persons notably guilty of this crime. No wonder that a common practice thereof doth fetch down public judgments; and that, as the prophets of old did proclaim, "because of swearing the land mourneth."

VIII. Further (passing over the special laws against it, the mischievous consequences of it, the sore punishments appointed to it), we may consider, that to common sense vain swearing is a very unreasonable and ill-favoured practice, greatly misbecoming any sober, worthy, or honest person; but especially most absurd and incongruous to a Christian.

For in ordinary conversation what needful or reasonable occasion can intervene of violating this command? If there come under discourse a matter of reason, which is evidently true and certain, then what need can there be of an oath to affirm it, it sufficing to expose it to light, or to propose the evidences for it? If an obscure or doubtful point come to be debated, it will not bear an oath; it will be a strange madness to dare, a great folly to hope the persuading it thereby. What were more ridiculous than to swear the truth of a demonstrable theorem? What more vain than so to assert a disputable problem: oaths (like wagers) are in such cases no arguments, except silliness in the users of them.

If a matter of history be started, then if a man be taken for honest, his word will pass for attestation without further assurance; but if his veracity or probity be doubted, his oath will not be relied on, especially when he doth obtrude it. For it was no less truly than acutely said by the old poet, Ουκ ανδρος ορκοι πιστις, αλλ' ορκων ανηρ, "The man doth not get credit from an oath, but an oath from the man." And a greater author, "An oath," saith St. Chrysostom, "doth not make a man credible; but the testimony of his life, and the exactness of his conversation, and a good repute. Many often have burst with swearing, and persuaded no man; others only nodding have deserved more belief than those who swore so mightily." Wherefore oaths, as they are frivolous coming from a person of little worth or conscience, so they are superfluous in the mouth of an honest and worthy person; yea, as they do not increase the credit of the former, so they may impair that of the latter.

"A good man," as Socrates did say, "should apparently so demean himself, that his word may be deemed more credible than an oath;" the constant tenour of his practice vouching for it, and giving it such weight, that no asseveration can further corroborate it.

He should τοις εργοις ευορκειν, "swear by his good deeds," and exhibit βιον αξιοπιστον, "a life deserving belief," as Clemens Alex. saith: so that no man should desire more from him than his bare assertion; but willingly should yield him the privilege which the Athenians granted to Xenocrates, that he should testify without swearing.

He should be like the Essenes, of whom Josephus saith, that everything spoken by them was more valid than an oath; whence they declined swearing.

He should so much confide in his own veracity and fidelity, and so much stand upon them, that he should not deign to offer any pledge for them, implying them to want confirmation.

"He should," as St. Jerome saith, "so love truth, that he should suppose himself to have sworn whatsoever he hath said;" and therefore should not be apt to heap another oath on his words.

Upon such accounts common reason directed even pagan wise men wholly to interdict swearing in ordinary conversation, or about petty matters, as an irrational and immoral practice, unworthy of sober and discreet persons. "Forbear swearing about any matter," said Plato, cited by Clem. Alex. "Avoid swearing, if you can, wholly," said Epictetus. "For money swear by no god, though you swear truly," said Socrates. And divers the like precepts occur in other heathens; the mention whereof may well serve to strike shame into many loose and vain people bearing the name of Christians.

Indeed, for a true and real Christian, this practice doth especially in a far higher degree misbecome him, upon considerations peculiar to his high calling and holy profession.

Plutarch telleth us that among the Romans the flamen of Jupiter was not permitted to swear, of which law among other reasons he assigned this: "Because it is not handsome that he to whom divine and greatest things are entrusted should be distrusted about small matters." The which reason may well be applied to excuse every Christian from it, who is a priest to the most High God, and hath the most celestial and important matters concredited to him; in comparison to which all other matters are very mean and inconsiderable. The dignity of his rank should render his word *verbum honoris*, passable without any further engagement. He hath opinions of things, he hath undertaken practices inconsistent with swearing. For he that firmly doth believe that God is ever present with him, and auditor and witness of all his discourse; he that is persuaded that a severe judgment shall pass on him, wherein he must give an account for every idle word which slippeth from him, and wherein, among other offenders, assuredly liars will be condemned to the burning lake; he that in a great Sacrament (once most solemnly taken, and frequently renewed) hath engaged and sworn, together with all other divine commandments, to observe those which most expressly do charge him to be exactly just, faithful, and veracious in all his words and deeds; who therefore should be ready to say with David, "I have sworn, and am steadfastly purposed to keep thy righteous judgments," to him every word hath the force of an oath; every lie, every breach of promise, every violation of faith doth involve perjury: for him to swear is false heraldry, an impertinent accumulation of one oath upon another; he of all men should disdain to allow that his words are not perfectly credible, that his promise is not secure, without being assured by an oath.

IX. Indeed, the practice of swearing greatly disparageth him that useth it, and derogateth from his credit upon divers accounts.

It signifieth (if it signifieth anything) that he doth not confide in his own reputation, and judgeth his own bare word not to deserve credit: for why, if he taketh his word to be good, doth he back it with asseverations? why, if he deemeth his own honesty to bear proof, doth he cite Heaven to warrant it?

"It is," saith St. Basil, "a very foul and silly thing for a man to accuse himself as unworthy of belief, and to proffer an oath for security."

By so doing a man doth authorise others to distrust him; for it can be no wrong to distrust him who doth not pretend to be a credible person, or that his saying alone may safely be taken: who, by suspecting that others are not satisfied with his simple assertion, implieth a reason known to himself for it.

It rendereth whatever he saith to be in reason suspicious, as discovering him void of conscience and discretion; for he that flatly against the rules of duty and reason will swear vainly, what can engage him to speak truly? He that is so loose in so clear and so considerable a point of obedience to God, how can he be supposed staunch in regard to any other? "It being," as Aristotle hath it, "the part of the same men to do ill things, and not to regard forswearing." It will at least constrain any man to suspect all his discourse of vanity and unadvisedness, seeing he plainly hath no care to bridle his tongue from so gross an offence.

It is strange, therefore, that any man of honour or honesty should not scorn, by such a practice, to shake his own credit, or to detract from the validity of his word; which should stand firm on itself, and not want any attestation to support it. It is a privilege of honourable persons that they are excused from swearing, and that their *verbum honoris* passeth in lieu of an oath: is it not then strange, that when others dispense with them, they should not dispense with themselves, but voluntarily degrade themselves, and with sin forfeit so noble a privilege?

X. To excuse these faults, the swearer will be forced to confess that his oaths are no more than waste and insignificant words, deprecating being taken for serious, or to be understood that he meaneth anything by them, but only that he useth them as expletive phrases, προς αναπληρωσιν λογου, to plump his speech, and fill up sentences. But such pleas do no more than suggest other faults of swearing, and good arguments against it; its impertinence, its abuse of speech, its disgracing the practiser of it in point of judgment and capacity. For so it is, oaths as they commonly pass are mere excrescences of speech, which do nothing but encumber and deform it; they so embellish discourse, as a wen or a scab do beautify a face, as a patch or a spot do adorn a garment.

To what purpose, I pray, is God's name hooked and haled into our idle talk? why should we so often mention Him, when we do not mean anything about Him? would it not, into every sentence to foist a dog or a horse, to intrude Turkish, or any barbarous gibberish, be altogether as proper and pertinent?

What do these superfluities signify, but that the venter of them doth little skill the use of speech, or the rule of conversation, but meaneth to sputter and prate anything without judgment or wit; that his invention is very barren, his fancy beggarly, craving the aid of any stuff to relieve it? One would think a man of sense should grudge to lend his ear, or incline his attention to such motley ragged discourse; that without nauseating he scarce should endure to observe men lavishing time, and squandering their breath so frivolously. 'Tis an affront to good company to pester it with such talk.

XI. But further, upon higher accounts this is a very uncivil and unmannerly practice.

Some vain persons take it for a genteel and graceful thing; a special accomplishment, a mark of fine breeding, a point of high gallantry; for who, forsooth, is the brave spark, the complete gentleman, the man of conversation and address, but he that hath the skill and confidence (O heavens! how mean a skill! how mad a confidence!) to lard every sentence with an oath or a curse, making bold at every turn to salute his Maker, or to summon Him in attestation of his tattle; not to say calling and challenging the Almighty to damn and destroy him? Such a conceit, I say, too many have of swearing, because a custom thereof, together with divers other fond and base qualities, hath prevailed among some people, bearing the name and garb of gentlemen.

But in truth, there is no practice more crossing the genuine nature of genteelness, or misbecoming persons well born and well bred; who should excel the rude vulgar in goodness, in courtesy, in nobleness of heart, in unwillingness to offend, and readiness to oblige those with whom they converse, in steady composedness of mind and manners, in disdaining to say or do any unworthy, any unhandsome things.

For this practice is not only a gross rudeness toward the main body of men, who justly reverence the name of God, and detest such an abuse thereof; not only further an insolent defiance of the common profession, the religion, the law of our country, which disalloweth and condemneth it, but it is very odious and offensive to any particular society or company, at least, wherein there is any sober person, any who retaineth a sense of goodness, or is anywise concerned for God's honour: for to any such person no language can be more disgustful; nothing can more grate his ears, or fret his heart, than to hear the sovereign object of his love and esteem so mocked and slighted; to see the law of his Prince so disloyally infringed, so contemptuously trampled on; to find his best Friend and Benefactor so outrageously abused. To give him the lie were a compliment, to spit in his face were an obligation, in comparison to this usage.

Wherefore 'tis a wonder that any person of rank, any that hath in him a spark of ingenuity, or doth at all pretend to good manners, should find in his heart or deign to comply with so scurvy a fashion: a fashion much more befitting the scum of the people than the flower of the gentry; yea, rather much below any man endued with a scrap of reason or a grain of goodness. Would we bethink ourselves, modest, sober, and pertinent discourse would appear far more generous and masculine than such mad hectoring the Almighty, such boisterous insulting over the received laws and general notions of mankind, such ruffianly swaggering against sobriety and goodness. If gentlemen would regard the virtues of their ancestors, the founders of their quality—that gallant courage and solid wisdom, that noble courtesy, which advanced their families and severed them from the vulgar—this degenerate wantonness and forbidness of language would return to the dunghill, or rather, which God grant, be quite banished from the world, the vulgar following their example.

XII. Further, the words of our Lord, when He forbade this practice, do suggest another consideration against it, deducible from the causes and sources of it; from whence it cometh, that men are so inclined or addicted thereto. "Let," saith He, "your communication be Yea, yea, Nay, nay; for whatsoever is more than these cometh of evil." The roots of it, He assureth us, are evil, and therefore the fruit cannot be good: it is no grape which groweth from thorns, or fig from thistles. Consult experience, and observe whence it doth proceed.

Sometimes it ariseth from exorbitant heats of spirit, or transports of unbridled passion. When a man is keenly peevish, or fiercely angry, or eagerly contentious, then he blustereth, and dischargeth his choler in most tragical strains; then he would fright the objects of his displeasure by the most violent expressions thereof. This is sometime alleged in excuse of rash swearing: I was provoked, the swearer will say, I was in passion; but it is strange that a bad cause should justify a bad effect, that one crime should warrant another, that what would spoil a good action should excuse a bad one.

Sometimes it proceedeth from arrogant conceit, and a tyrannical humour; when a man fondly admireth his own opinion, and affecting to impose it on others, is thence moved to thwack it on with lusty asseverations.

Sometimes it issueth from wantonness and levity of mind, disposing a man to sport with anything, how serious, how grave, how sacred and venerable soever.

Sometimes its rise is from stupid inadvertency, or heady precipitancy; when the man doth not heed what he saith, or consider the nature and consequence of his words, but snatcheth any expression which cometh next, or which his roving fancy doth offer, for want of that caution of the psalmist, "I said, I will take heed to my ways, that I sin not with my tongue; I will keep my mouth with a bridle, while the wicked is before me."

Sometimes (alas! how often in this miserable age!) it doth spring from profane boldness; when men design to put affronts on religion, and to display their scorn and spite against conscience, affecting the reputation of stout blades, of gallant hectors, of resolute giants, who dare do anything, who are not afraid to defy Heaven, and brave God Almighty Himself.

Sometimes it is derived from apish imitation, or a humour to comply with a fashion current among vain and dissolute persons.

It always doth come from a great defect in conscience, of reverence to God, of love to goodness, of discretion and sober regard to the welfare of a man's soul.

From such evidently vicious and unworthy sources it proceedeth, and therefore must needs be very culpable. No good, no wise man can like actions drawn from such principles. Further —

XIII. This offence may be particularly aggravated by considering that it hath no strong temptation alluring to it, that it yieldeth no sensible advantage, that it most easily may be avoided or corrected.

"Every sin," saith St. Chrysostom, "hath not the same punishment; but those things which may easily be reformed do bring on us greater punishment:" and what can be more easy than to reform this fault? "Tell me," saith he, "what difficulty, what sweat, what art, what hazard, what more doth it require beside a little care" to abstain wholly from it? It is but willing, or resolving on it, and it is instantly done; for there is not any natural inclination disposing to it, any strong appetite to detain us under its power.

It gratifieth no sense, it yieldeth no profit, it procureth no honour; for the sound of it is not very melodious, and no man surely did ever get an estate by it, or was preferred to dignity for it. It rather to any good ear maketh a horrid and jarring noise; it rather with the best part of the world produceth displeasure, damage, and disgrace. What therefore, beside monstrous vanity and unaccountable perverseness, should hold men so devoted thereto?

Surely of all dealers in sin the swearer is palpably the silliest, and maketh the worst bargains for himself, for he sinneth gratis, and, like those in the prophet, "selleth his soul for nothing." An epicure hath some reason to allege, an extortioner is a man of wisdom, and acteth prudently in comparison to him; for they enjoy some pleasure, or acquire some gain here, in lieu of their salvation hereafter, but this fondling offendeth Heaven, and abandoneth happiness, he knoweth not why or for what. He hath not so much as the common plea of human infirmity to excuse him; he can hardly say that he was tempted thereto by any bait.

A fantastic humour possesseth him of spurning at piety and soberness; he inconsiderately followeth a herd of wild fops, he affecteth to play the ape. What more than this can he say for himself?

XIV. Finally, let us consider that as we ourselves, with all our members and powers, were chiefly designed and framed to glorify our Maker, the which to do is indeed the greatest perfection and noblest privilege of our nature, so our tongue and speaking faculty were given to us to declare our admiration and reverence of Him, to exhibit our due love and gratitude toward Him, to profess our trust and confidence in Him, to celebrate His praises, to avow His benefits, to address our supplications to Him, to maintain all kinds of devotional intercourse with Him, to propagate our knowledge, fear, love, and obedience to Him, in all such ways to promote His honour and service. This is the most proper, worthy, and due use of our tongue, for which it was created, to which it is dedicated, from whence it becometh, as it is so often styled, our glory, and the best member that we have; that whereby we excel all creatures here below, and whereby we are no less discriminated from them, than by our reason; that whereby we consort with the blessed angels above in the distinct utterance of praise and communication of glory to our Creator. Wherefore, applying this to any impious discourse with which to profane God's blessed name, with this to violate His holy commands, with this to unhallow His sacred ordinance, with this to offer dishonour and indignity to Him, is a most unnatural abuse, a horrid ingratitude toward Him.

It is that indeed whereby we render this noble organ incapable of any good use. For how, as the excellent father doth often urge, can we pray to God for mercies, or praise God for His benefits, or heartily confess our sins, or cheerfully partake of the holy mysteries, with a mouth defiled by impious oaths, with a heart guilty of so heinous disobedience.

Likewise, whereas a secondary very worthy use of our speech is to promote the good of our neighbour, and especially to edify him in piety, according to that wholesome precept of the Apostle, "Let no corrupt communication proceed out of your mouth, but that which is good to the use of edifying, that it may administer grace unto the hearers." The practice of swearing is an abuse very contrary to that good purpose, serving to corrupt our neighbour, and to instil into him a contempt of religion; or however grievously to scandalise him.

XV. I shall add but two words more. One is, that we would seriously consider that our Blessed Saviour, who loved us so dearly, who did and suffered so much for us, who redeemed us by His blood, who said unto us, "If ye love Me, keep My commandments," He thus positively hath enjoined, "But I say unto you, Swear not at all;" and how then can we find in our heart directly to thwart His word.

The other is, that we would lay to heart the reason whereby St. James doth enforce the point, and the sting in the close of our text, wherewith I conclude: "But above all things, my brethren, swear not, neither by heaven, neither by the earth, neither by any other oath; but let your yea be yea, and your nay nay, lest ye fall into condemnation," or, "lest ye fall under damnation." From the which infinite mischief, and from all sin that may cause it, God in mercy deliver us through our Blessed Redeemer Jesus, to whom for ever be all glory and praise.

OF EVIL-SPEAKING IN GENERAL.

"To speak evil of no man." — Titus iii. 2.

These words do imply a double duty; one incumbent on teachers, another on the people who are to be instructed by them.

The teacher's duty appeareth from reflecting on the words of the context, which govern these, and make them up an entire sentence: put them in mind, or, rub up their memory to do thus. It is St. Paul's injunction to Titus, a bishop and pastor of the Church, that he should admonish the people committed to his care and instruction, as of other great duties (of yielding obedience to magistrates, of behaving themselves peaceably, of practising meekness and equity towards all men, of being readily disposed to every good work), so particularly of this, μηδενα βλασφημειν, to revile or speak evil of no man.

Whence it is apparent that this is one of the principal duties that preachers are obliged to mind people of, and to press upon them. And if this were needful then, when charity, kindled by such instructions and examples, was so lively; when Christians, by their sufferings, were so inured to meekness and patience; even every one, for the honour of his religion, and the safety of his person, was concerned in all respects to demean himself innocently and inoffensively; then is it now especially requisite, when (such engagements and restraints being taken off, love being cooled, persecution being extinct, the tongue being set loose from all extraordinary curbs) the transgression of this duty is grown so prevalent and rife, that evil-speaking is almost as common as speaking, ordinary conversation extremely abounding therewith, that ministers should discharge their office in dehorting and dissuading from it.

Well indeed it were, if by their example of using mild and moderate discourse, of abstaining from virulent invectives, tauntings, and scoffings, good for little but to inflame anger, and infuse ill-will, they would lead men to good practice of this sort: for no examples can be so wholesome, or so mischievous to this purpose, as those which come down from the pulpit, the place of edification, backed with special authority and advantage.

However, it is to preachers a ground of assurance and matter of satisfaction, that in pressing this duty they shall perform their duty: their text being not so much of their own choosing, as given them by St. Paul; they can surely scarce find a better to discourse upon: it cannot be a matter of small moment or use, which this great master and guide so expressly directeth us to insist upon. And to the observance of his precept, so far as concerneth me, I shall immediately apply myself.

It is then the duty of all Christian people (to be taught and pressed on them) not to reproach, or speak evil of any man. The which duty, for your instruction, I shall first endeavour somewhat to explain, declaring its import and extent; then, for your further edification, I shall inculcate it, proposing several inducements persuasive to the observance of it.

I. For explication, we may first consider the object of it, no man; then the act itself, which is prohibited, to blaspheme, that is, to reproach, to revile, or (as we have it rendered) to speak evil.

No man. St. Paul questionless did especially mean hereby to hinder the Christians at that time from reproaching the Jews and the pagans among whom they lived, men in their lives very wicked and corrupt, men in opinion extremely dissenting from them, men who greatly did hate, and cruelly did persecute them; of whom therefore they had mighty provocations and temptations to speak ill; their judgment of the persons, and their resentment of injuries, making it difficult to abstain from doing so. Whence by a manifest analogy may be inferred that the object of duty is very large, indeed universal and unlimited: that we must forbear reproach not only against pious and virtuous persons, against persons of our own judgment or party, against those who never did harm or offend us, against our relations, our friends, our benefactors, in respect of whom there is no ground or temptation of evil-speaking; but even against the most unworthy and wicked persons, against those who most differ in opinion and practice from us, against those who never did oblige us, yea, those who have most disobliged us, even against our most bitter and spiteful enemies. There is no exception or excuse to be admitted from the quality, state, relation, or demeanour of men; the duty (according to the proper sense, or due qualifications and limits of the act) doth extend to all men: for, "Speak evil of no man."

As for the act, it may be inquired what the word βλασφημειν (to blaspheme) doth import. I answer, that it is to vent words concerning any person which do signify in us ill-opinion, or contempt, anger, hatred, enmity conceived in our minds towards him; which are apt in him to kindle wrath, and breed ill-blood towards us; which tend to beget in others that hear ill-conceit or ill-will towards him; which are much destructive of his reputation, prejudicial to his interests, productive of damage or mischief to him. It is otherwise in Scripture termed λοιδορειν, to rail or revile, (to use bitter and ignominious language); υβριζειν, to speak contumeliously; φερειν βλασφημον κρισιν, to bring railing accusation (or reproachful censure); καταλαλειν, to use obloquy, or detraction; καταρασθαι, to curse, that is, to speak words importing that we do wish ill to a person.

Such is the language we are prohibited to use. To which purpose we may observe that whereas, in our conversation and commerce with men, there do frequently often occur occasions to speak of men and to men words apparently disadvantageous to them, expressing our dissent in opinion from them, or a dislike in us of their proceedings, we may do this in different ways and terms; some of them gentle and moderate, signifying no ill mind or disaffection towards them; others harsh and sharp, arguing height of disdain, disgust, or despite, whereby we bid them defiance, and show that we mean to exasperate them. Thus, telling a man that we differ in judgment from him, or conceive him not to be in the right, and calling him a liar, a deceiver, a fool, saying that he doeth amiss, taketh a wrong course, transgresseth the rule, and calling him dishonest, unjust, wicked, to omit more odious and provoking names, unbecoming this place, and not deserving our notice, are several ways of expressing the same things whereof the latter, in relating passages concerning our neighbour, or in debating cases with him, is prohibited: for thus the words reproaching, reviling, railing, cursing, and the like do signify, and thus our Lord Himself doth explain them in His divine sermon, wherein he doth enact this law: "Whosoever," saith He, "shall say to his brother, Raca" (that is, vain man, or liar), "shall be in danger of the council; but whosoever shall say, Thou fool, shall be in danger of hell-fire;" that is, he rendereth himself liable to a strict account, and to severe condemnation before God, who useth contemptuous and contumelious expressions towards his neighbour, in proportion to the malignity of such expressions.

The reason of things also doth help to explain those words, and to show why they are prohibited because those harsh terms are needless, mild words serving as well to express the same things: because they are commonly unjust, loading men with greater defect or blame than they can be proved to deserve, or their actions do import; for every man that speaketh falsehood is not therefore a liar, every man that erreth is not thence a fool, every man that doeth amiss is not consequently dishonest or wicked; the secret intentions and habitual dispositions of men not being always to be collected from their outward actions; because they are uncharitable, signifying that we entertain the worst opinions of men, and make the worst construction of their doings, and are disposed to show them no favour or kindness: because, also, they produce mischievous effects, such as spring from the worst passions raised by them.

This in gross is the meaning of the precept. But since there are some other precepts seeming to clash with this; since there are cases wherein we are allowed to use the harsher sort of terms, there are great examples in appearance thwarting this rule; therefore it may be requisite for determining the limits of our duty, and distinguishing it from transgression, that such exceptions or restrictions should be somewhat declared.

1. First, then, we may observe that it may be allowable to persons in anywise concerned in the prosecution or administration of jus-

tice, to speak words which in private intercourse would be reproachful. A witness may impeach of crimes hurtful to justice, or public tranquillity; a judge may challenge, may rebuke, may condemn an offender in proper terms (or forms of speech prescribed by law), although most disgraceful and distasteful to the guilty: for it belongeth to the majesty of public justice to be bold, blunt, severe; little regarding the concerns or passions of particular persons, in comparison to the public welfare.

A testimony, therefore, or sentence against a criminal, which materially is a reproach, and morally would be such in a private mouth, is not yet formally so according to the intent of this rule. For practices of this kind, which serve the exigencies of justice, are not to be interpreted as proceeding from anger, hatred, revenge, any bad passion or humour; but in way of needful discipline for God's service, and common benefit of men. It is not, indeed, so much the minister of justice, as God Himself, our absolute Lord; as the Sovereign, God's representative, acting in the public behalf; as the commonwealth itself, who by His mouth do rebuke the obnoxious person.

2. God's ministers in religious affairs, to whom the care of men's instruction and edification is committed, are enabled to inveigh against sin and vice, whoever consequentially may be touched thereby: yea, sometimes it is their duty with severity and sharpness to reprove particular persons, not only privately, but publicly, for their correction, and for the edification of others.

Thus St. Paul directeth Timothy: "Them that sin" (notoriously and scandalously, he meaneth), "rebuke before all, that others may fear:" that is, in a manner apt to make impression on the minds of the hearers, so as to scare them from like offences. And to Titus he writes, "Rebuke them sharply, that they may be found in the faith." And, "Cry aloud, spare not, lift up thy voice like a trumpet, and show my people their transgressions, and the house of Jacob their sins," saith the Lord to the prophet. Such are the charges and commissions laid on and granted to His messengers.

Thus we may observe that God's prophets of old, St. John the Baptist, our Lord Himself, the holy apostles did in terms most vehement and biting reprove the age in which they lived, and some particular persons in them. The prophets are full of declamations and invectives against the general corruption of their times, and against the particular manners of some persons in them. "Ah, sinful nation; people laden with iniquity, a seed of evil-doers, children that are corrupters! They are all adulterers, an assembly of treacherous men; and they bend their tongues like their bow for lies. Thy princes are rebellious and companions of thieves; every one loveth gifts, and followeth after rewards: they judge not the fatherless, neither doth the cause of the widow come before them. The prophets prophesy falsely, and the priests rule by their means. As troops of robbers wait for a man, so the company of priests murder in the way by consent, and commit lewdness." Such is their style commonly. St. John the Baptist calleth the Scribes and Pharisees a "generation of vipers." Our Saviour speaketh of them in the same terms; calleth them an "evil and adulterous generation, serpents, and children of vipers. Hypocrites, painted sepulchres, obscure graves (μνημεια αδηλα), blind guides; fools and blind, children of the devil." St. Paul likewise calleth the schismatical heretical teachers "dogs, false apostles, evil and deceitful workers, men of corrupt minds, reprobates and abominable." With the like colours do St. Peter, St. Jude, and other apostles paint them. Which sort of speeches are to be supposed to proceed, not from private passion or design, but out of holy zeal for God's honour, and from earnest charity towards men, for to work their amendment and common edification. They were uttered also by special wisdom and peculiar order; from God's authority, and in His name; so that, as God by them is said to preach, to entreat, to warn, and to exhort, so by them also He may be said to reprehend and reproach.

3. Even private persons in due season, with discretion and temper, may reprove others, whom they observe to commit sin, or follow bad courses, out of charitable design, and with hope to reclaim them. This was an office of charity imposed anciently even upon the Jews; much more doth it lie upon Christians, who are obliged more earnestly to tender the spiritual good of those who by the stricter and more holy bands of brotherhood are allied to them. "Thou shalt not hate thy brother; thou shalt in any wise rebuke thy neighbour, and not suffer sin upon him," was a precept of the old law: and, νουθετειν ατακτους, to admonish the disorderly, is an evangelical

rule. Such persons we are enjoined to shun and decline; but first we must endeavour by sober advice and admonition to reclaim them; we must not thus reject them till they appear contumacious and incorrigible, refusing to hear us, or becoming deaf to reproof. This, although it necessarily doth include setting out their faults, and charging blame on them (answerable to their offences), is not the culpable reproach here meant, it being needful towards a wholesome effect, and proceeding from charitable intention.

4. Some vehemency, some smartness and sharpness of speech may sometimes be used in defence of truth, and impugning errors of bad consequence; especially when it concerneth the interest of truth, that the reputation and authority of its adversaries should somewhat be abased or abated. If by partial opinion or reverence towards them, however begotten in the minds of men, they strive to overbear or discountenance a good cause, their faults (so far as truth permitteth and need requireth) may be detected and displayed. For this cause particularly may we presume our Lord (otherwise so meek in His temper, and mild in His carriage towards all men) did characterise the Jewish scribes in such terms, that their authority, being then so prevalent with the people, might not prejudice the truth, and hinder the efficacy of His doctrine. This is part of that επαγωνιζεσθαι τη πιστει, that duty of contending earnestly for the faith, which is incumbent on us.

5. It may be excusable upon particular emergent occasions, with some heat of language to express dislike of notorious wickedness. As our Lord doth against the perverse incredulity and stupidity in the Pharisees, their profane misconstruction of His words and actions, their malicious opposing truth, and obstructing His endeavours in God's service. As St. Peter did to Simon Magus, telling him that he was in the gall of bitterness, and in the bond of iniquity. As St. Paul to Elymas the sorcerer, when he withstood him, and desired to turn away the Deputy Sergius from the faith; "O," said he, stirred with a holy zeal and indignation, "thou full of all subtilty and all mischief, thou child of the devil, thou enemy of all righteousness, wilt thou not cease to pervert the right ways of the Lord?" The same spirit which enabled him to inflict a sore punishment on that wicked wretch, did prompt him to use that sharp language towards him; unquestionably deserved, and seasonably pronounced. As also

when the high priest commanded him illegally and unjustly to be misused, that speech from a mind justly sensible of such outrage broke forth, "God shall smite thee, thou whited wall." So when St. Peter presumptuously would have dissuaded our Lord from compliance with God's will, in undergoing those crosses which were appointed to Him by God's decree, our Lord calleth him Satan; . . . . "Υπαγε Σατανα, "Avaunt, Satan, thou art an offence unto Me; for thou savourest not the things that be of God, but those that are of men."

These sort of speeches, issuing from just and honest indignation, are sometimes excusable, oftentimes commendable; especially when they come from persons eminent in authority, of notable integrity, endued with special measures of Divine grace, of wisdom, of goodness; such as cannot be suspected of intemperate anger, of ill-nature, of ill-will, or of ill-design.

In such cases as are above mentioned, a sort of evil-speaking about our neighbour may be allowable or excusable. But, for fear of overdoing, great caution and temper is to be used; and we should never apply any such limitations as cloaks to palliate unjust or uncharitable dealing. Generally it is more advisable to suppress such eruptions of passion than to vent it; for seldom passion hath not inordinate motions joined with it, or tendeth to good ends. And, however, it will do well to reflect on those cases, and to remark some particulars about them.

First, we may observe that in all these cases all possible moderation, equity, and candour are to be used; so that no ill-speaking be practised beyond what is needful or convenient. Even in prosecution of offences, the bounds of truth, of equity, of humanity and clemency are not to be transgressed. A judge must not lay on the most criminal person more blame or contumely than the case will bear, or than serveth the designs of justice. However our neighbour doth incur the calamities of sin and of punishment, we must not be insolent or contemptuous towards him. So we may learn by that law of Moses, backed with a notable reason: "And it shall be, if the wicked man be worthy to be beaten, that the judge cause him to lie down, and to be beaten before his face, according to his fault by a certain number. Forty stripes he may give him, and not exceed; lest if he should exceed, and beat him above those stripes, then thy brother should seem vile unto thee." Whence appears that we should be careful of not vilifying an offender beyond measure. And how mildly governors should proceed in the administration of justice, the example of Joshua may teach us, who thus examineth Achan, the cause of so great mischief to the public: "My son, give, I pray thee, glory to the Lord God of Israel, and make confession unto Him; and tell me now what thou hast done, and hide it not from me." "My son;" what compellation could be more benign and kind? "I pray thee;" what language could be more courteous and gentle? "give glory to God, and make confession;" what words could be more inoffensively pertinent? And when he sentenced that great malefactor, the cause of so much mischief, this was all he said, "Why hast thou troubled us? the Lord will trouble thee;" words void of contumely or insulting, containing only a close intimation of the cause, and a simple declaration of the event he was to undergo.

Secondly, likewise ministers, in the taxing sin and sinners, are to proceed with great discretion and caution, with much gentleness and meekness; signifying a tender pity of their infirmities, charitable desires for their good, the best opinion of them, and the best hopes for them, that may consist with any reason; according to those apostolical rules: "Brethren, if a man be overtaken in a fault, ye which are spiritual, restore such an one in the spirit of meekness; considering thyself, lest thou also be tempted;" and, "We that are strong ought to bear the infirmities of the weak, and not to please ourselves:" and, more expressly, "A servant of the Lord must not fight, but be gentle toward all, apt to teach, patient, in meekness instructing those that oppose themselves." Thus did St. Peter temper his reproof of Simon Magus with this wholesome and comfortable advice: "Repent, therefore, from this thy wickedness, and pray God if perhaps the thought of thine heart may be forgiven thee."

Thirdly, as for fraternal censure and reproof of faults (when it is just and expedient to use it), ordinarily the calmest and mildest way is the most proper, and most likely to obtain good success; it commonly doth in a more kindly manner convey the sense thereof into the heart, and therein more powerfully worketh remorse, than the fierce and harsh way. Clearly to show a man his fault, with the reason proving it such, so that he becometh thoroughly convinced of it, is sufficient to breed in him regret, and to shame him before his own mind: to do more (in way of aggravation, of insulting on him, of inveighing against him), as it doth often not well consist with humanity, so it is seldom consonant to discretion, if we do, as we ought, seek his health and amendment. Humanity requireth that when we undertake to reform our neighbour, we should take care not to deform him (not to discourage or displease him more than is necessary); when we would correct his manners, that we should also consider his modesty, and consult his reputation; "*curam agentes,*" as Seneca speaketh, "*non tantum salutis, sed et honestf cicatricis*" (having care not only to heal the wound, but to leave a comely scar behind). "Be," adviseth St. Austin, "so displeased with iniquity, as to consider and consult humanity;" for, "Zeal void of humanity is not," saith St. Chrysostom, "zeal, but rather animosity; and reproof not mixed with good-will appeareth a kind of malignity." We should so rebuke those who, by frailty or folly incident to mankind, have fallen into misdemeanours, that they may perceive we do sincerely pity their ill case, and tender their good; that we mean not to upbraid their weakness or insult upon their misfortune; that we delight not to inflict on them more grief than is plainly needful and unavoidable; that we are conscious and sensible of our own obnoxiousness to the like slips or falls, and do consider that we also may be tempted, and being tempted, may be overborne. This they cannot perceive or be persuaded of, except we temper our speech with benignity and mildness. Such speech prudence also dictateth, as most useful and hopeful for producing the good ends honest reprehension doth aim at; it mollifieth and it melteth a stubborn heart, it subdueth and winneth a perverse will, it healeth distempered affections. Whereas roughly handling is apt to defeat or obstruct the cure: rubbing the sore doth tend to exasperate and inflame it. Harsh speech rendereth advice odious and unsavoury; driveth from it and depriveth it of efficacy; it turneth regret for a fault into displeasure and disdain against the reprover; it looks not like the dealing of a kind friend, but like the persecution of a spiteful enemy; it seemeth rather an ebullition of gall, or a defluxion from rancour, than an expression of good-will; the offender will take it for a needless and pitiless tormenting, or for a proud and tyrannical domineering over him. He that can bear a friendly touch, will not endure to be lashed with angry and reproachful words. In fine, all reproof ought to be seasoned with discretion, with candour, with moderation, and meekness.

Fourthly, likewise in defence of truth, and maintenance of a good cause, we may observe that commonly the fairest language is most proper and advantageous, and that reproachful or foul terms are most improper and prejudicial. A calm and meek way of discoursing doth much advantage a good cause, as arguing the patron thereof to have confidence in the cause itself, and to rely upon his strength: that he is in a temper fit to apprehend it himself, and to maintain it; that he propoundeth it as a friend, wishing the hearer for his own good to follow it, leaving him the liberty to judge, and choose for himself. But rude speech, and contemptuous reflections on persons, as they do signify nothing to the question, so they commonly bring much disadvantage and damage to the cause, creating mighty prejudices against it; they argue much impotency in the advocate, and consequently little strength in what he maintains; that he is little able to judge well, and altogether unapt to teach others; they intimate a diffidence in himself concerning his cause, and that, despairing to maintain it by reason, he seeks to uphold it by passion; that not being able to convince by fair means, he would bear down by noise and clamour: that not skilling to get his suit quietly, he would extort it by force, obtruding his conceits violently as an enemy, or imposing them arbitrarily as a tyrant. Thus doth he really disparage and slur his cause, however good and defensible in itself.

A modest and friendly style doth suit truth; it, like its author, doth usually reside (not in the rumbling wind, nor in the shaking earthquake, nor in the raging fire, but) in the small still voice; sounding in this, it is most audible, most penetrant, and most effectual; thus propounded, it is willingly hearkened to: for men have no aversion from hearing those who seem to love them, and wish them well. It is easily conceived, no prejudice or passion clouding the apprehensive faculties; it is readily embraced, no animosity withstanding or obstructing it. It is the sweetness of the lips, which, as the wise man telleth us, increaseth learning; disposing a man to hear lessons of good doctrine, rendering him capable to understand them, insinuating and impressing them upon the mind; the affections being thereby unlocked, the passage becomes open to the reason.

But it is plainly a preposterous method of instructing, of deciding controversies, of begetting peace, to vex and anger those concerned by ill language. Nothing surely doth more hinder the efficacy of discourse, and prevent conviction, than doth this course, upon many obvious accounts. It doth first put in a strong bar to attention: for no man willingly doth afford an ear to him whom he conceiveth disaffected towards him: which opinion harsh words infallibly will produce; no man can expect to hear truth from him whom he apprehendeth disordered in his own mind, whom he seeth rude in his proceedings, whom he taketh to be unjust in his dealing; as men certainly will take those to be, who presume to revile others for using their own judgment freely, and dissenting from them in opinion. Again, this course doth blind the hearer's mind, so that he cannot discern what he that pretends to instruct him doth mean, or how he doth assert his doctrine. Truth will not be discerned through the smoke of wrathful expressions; right being defaced by foul language will not appear, passion being excited will not suffer a man to perceive the sense or the force of an argument. The will also thereby is hardened and hindered from submitting to truth. In such a case, *non persuadebis, etiamsi persuaseris*; although you stop his mouth, you cannot subdue his heart; although he can no longer fight, yet he never will yield: animosity raised by such usage rendereth him invincibly obstinate in his conceits and courses. Briefly, from this proceeding men become unwilling to mark, unfit to apprehend, indisposed to embrace any good instruction or advice; it maketh them indocile and intractable, averse from better instruction, pertinacious in their opinions, and refractory in their ways.

"Every man," saith the wise man, "shall kiss his lips that giveth a right answer;" but no man surely will be ready to kiss those lips which are embittered with reproach, or defiled with dirty language.

It is said of Pericles, that with thundering and lightning he put Greece into confusion; such discourse may serve to confound things, it seldom tendeth to compose them. If reason will not pierce, rage will scarce avail to drive it in. Satirical virulency may vex men sorely, but it hardly ever soundly converts them. "Few become wiser or better by ill words." Children may be frightened into compliance by loud and severe reprimands; but men are to be allured by rational persuasion backed with courteous usage; they may be sweetly drawn, they cannot be violently driven to change their judgment and practice. Whence that advice of the apostle, "With meekness instruct those that oppose themselves," doth no less savour of wisdom than of goodness.

Fifthly, as for examples of extraordinary persons, which in some cases do seem to authorise the practice of evil-speaking, we may consider that, as they had especial commission enabling them to do some things beyond ordinary standing rules, wherein they are not to be imitated: as they had especial illumination and direction, which preserved them from swerving in particular cases from truth and equity; so the tenor of their life did evidence that it was the glory of God, the good of men, the necessity of the case, which moved them to it. And of them also we may observe, that on divers occasions (yea, generally, whenever only their private credit or interest was concerned), although grievously provoked, they did out of meekness, patience, and charity, wholly forbear reproachful speech. Our Saviour, who sometimes upon special reason in His discourses used such harsh words, yet when He was most spitefully accused, reproached, and persecuted, did not open His mouth, or return one angry word: "Being reviled, He did not," as St. Peter, proposing His example to us, telleth us, "revile again; suffering, He did not threaten." He used the softest language to Judas, to the soldiers, to Pilate and Herod, to the priests, etc. And the apostles, who sometimes inveigh so zealously against the opposers and perverters of truth, did in their private conversation and demeanour strictly observe their own rules, of abstinence from reproach: "Being reviled, we bless; being persecuted, we suffer it;" so doth St. Paul represent their practice. And in reason we should rather follow them in this their ordinary course, than in their extraordinary sallies of practice.

In fine, however in some cases and circumstances the matter may admit such exceptions, so that all language disgraceful to our neighbour is not ever culpable; yet the cases are so few and rare in comparison, the practice commonly so dangerous and ticklish, that worthily forbearing to reproach doth bear the style of a general rule;

and particularly (for clearer direction) we are in the following cases obliged carefully to shun it; or in speaking about our neighbour we must observe these cautions.

1. We should never in severe terms inveigh against any man without reasonable warrant, or presuming upon a good call and commission thereto. As every man should not assume to himself the power of administering justice (of trying, sentencing, and punishing offenders), so must not every man take upon him to speak against those who seem to do ill; which is a sort of punishment, including the infliction of smart and damage upon the persons concerned. Every man hath indeed a commission, in due place and season, with discretion and moderation to admonish his neighbour offending; but otherwise to speak ill of him, no private man hath just right or authority, and therefore, in presuming to do it, he is disorderly and irregular, trespassing beyond his bounds, usurping an undue power to himself.

2. We should never speak ill of any man without apparent just cause. It must be just; we must not reproach men for things innocent or indifferent; for not concurring in disputable opinions with us, for not complying with our humour, for not serving our interest, for not doing anything to which they are not obliged, or for using their liberty in any case: it must be at least some considerable fault, which we can so much as tax. It must also be clear and certain, notorious and palpable; for to speak ill upon slender conjectures, or doubtful suspicions, is full of iniquity. "Οσα ουκ οιδασι, βλασφημουσι, "They rail at things which they know not," is part of those wicked men's character, whom St. Jude doth so severely reprehend. If, indeed, these conditions being wanting, we presume to reproach any man, we do therein no less than slander him; which to do is unlawful in any case, is in truth a most diabolical and detestable crime. To impose odious names and characters on any person, which he deserveth not, or without ground of truth, is to play the devil; and hell itself scarce will own a fouler practice.

3. We should not cast reproach upon any man without some necessary reason. In charity (that charity which "covereth all sins," which "covereth a multitude of sins") we are bound to connive at the defects, and to conceal the faults of our brethren; to extenuate

and excuse them, when apparent, so far as we may in truth and equity. We must not therefore ever produce them to light, or prosecute them with severity, except very needful occasion urgeth—such as is the glory and service of God, the maintenance of truth, the vindication of innocence, the preservation of public justice and peace; the amendment of our neighbour himself, or securing others from contagion. Barring such reasons (really being, not affectedly pretended), we are bound not so much as to disclose, as to touch our neighbour's faults; much more, not to blaze them about, not to exaggerate them by vehement invectives.

4. We should never speak ill of any man beyond measure; be the cause never so just, the occasion never so necessary, we should yet nowise be immoderate therein, exceeding the bounds prescribed by truth, equity, and humanity. We should never speak worse of any man whatever than he certainly deserveth, according to the most favourable construction of his doings; never more than the cause absolutely requireth. We should rather be careful to fall short of what in rigorous truth might be said against him, than in the least to pass beyond it. The best cause had better seem to suffer a little by our reservedness in its defence, than any man be wronged by our aspersing him; for God, the patron of truth and right, is ever able to secure them without the succour of our unjust and uncharitable dealing. The contrary practice hath indeed within it a spice of slander, that is, of the worst iniquity.

5. We must never speak ill of any man out of bad principles, or for bad ends.

No sudden or rash anger should instigate us thereto. For, "Let all bitterness, and wrath, and anger, and clamour, and evil-speaking be put away from you, with all malice," is the apostolical precept; they are all associates and kindred, which are to be cast away together. Such anger itself is culpable, as a work of the flesh, and therefore to be suppressed; and all its brood therefore is also to be smothered; the daughter of such a mother cannot be legitimate. "The wrath of man worketh not the righteousness of God."

We must not speak ill out of inveterate hatred or ill-will. For this murderous, this viperous disposition should itself be rooted out of our hearts: whatever issueth from it cannot be otherwise than very bad; it must be a poisonous breath that exhaleth from that foul source.

We must not be provoked thereto by any revengeful disposition, or rancorous spleen, in regard to any injuries or discourtesies received. For, as we must not revenge ourselves, or render evil in any other way, so particularly not in this, which is commonly the special instance expressly prohibited. "Render not evil for evil," saith St. Peter, "nor railing for railing; but contrariwise bless," or speak well; and "Bless them," saith the Lord, "which curse you;" "Bless," saith St. Paul, "and curse not."

We must not also do it out of contempt; for we are not to slight our brethren in our hearts. No man really, considering what he is, whence he came, how he is related, what he is capable of, can be despicable. Extreme naughtiness is indeed contemptible; but the unhappy person that is engaged therein is rather to be pitied than despised. However, charity bindeth us to stifle contemptuous motions of heart, and not to vent them in vilifying expression. Particularly, it is a barbarous practice, out of contempt to reproach persons for natural imperfections, for meanness of condition, for unlucky disasters, for any involuntary defects; this being indeed to reproach mankind, unto which such things are incident; to reproach Providence, from the disposal whereof they do proceed. "Whoso mocketh the poor, despiseth his Maker," saith the wise man; and the same may be said of him that reproachfully mocketh him that is dull in parts, deformed in body, weak in health or strength, defective in any such way.

Likewise we must not speak ill out of envy; because others do excel us in any good quality, or exceed us in fortune. To harbour this base and ugly disposition in our minds is unworthy of a man (who should delight in all good springing up anywhere, and befalling any man, naturally allied unto him); it is most unworthy of a Christian, who should tender his brother's good as his own, and rejoice with those that rejoice. From thence to be drawn to cast reproach upon any man, is horrible and heinous wickedness.

Neither should we ever use reproach as a means of compassing any design we do affect or aim at; 'tis an unwarrantable engine of raising us to wealth, dignity, or repute. To grow by the diminution, to rise by the depression, to shine by the eclipse of others, to build a fortune upon the ruins of our neighbour's reputation, is that which no honourable mind can affect, no honest man will endeavour. Our own wit, courage, and industry, managed with God's assistance and blessing, are sufficient, and only lawful instruments of prosecuting honest enterprises; we need not, we must not instead of them employ our neighbour's disgrace; no worldly good is worth purchasing at such a rate, no project worth achieving by such foul ways.

Neither should we out of malignity, to cherish or gratify ill humour, use this practice. It is observable of some persons, that not out of any formed displeasure, grudge, or particular disaffection, nor out of any particular design, but merely out of a κακοηθεια, an ill disposition, springing up from nature, or contracted by use, they are apt to carp at any action, and with sharp reproach to bite any man that comes in their way, thereby feeding and soothing that evil inclination. But as this inhuman and currish humour should be corrected, and extirpated from our hearts; so should the issues thereof at our mouths be stopped; the bespattering our neighbour's good name should never afford any satisfaction or delight unto us.

Nor out of wantonness should we speak ill, for our divertisement or sport. For our neighbour's reputation is too great and precious a thing to be played with, or offered up to sport; we are very foolish in so disvaluing it, very naughty in so misusing it. Our wits are very barren, our brains are ill furnished with store of knowledge, if we can find no other matter of conversation.

Nor out of negligence and inadvertency should we sputter out reproachful speech; shooting ill words at rovers, or not regarding who stands in our way. Among all temerities this is one of the most noxious, and therefore very culpable.

In fine, we should never speak concerning our neighbour from any other principle than charity, or to any other intent but what is charitable; such as tendeth to his good, or at least is consistent therewith. "Let all your things," saith St. Paul, "be done in charity;" and words are most of the *things* we do concerning our neighbour, wherein we may express charity. In all our speeches, therefore, touching him, we should plainly show that we have a care of his reputation, that we tender his interest, that we even desire his content and repose. Even when reason and need do so require that we should disclose and reprehend his faults, we may, we should by the manner and scope of our speech signify thus much. Which rule, were it observed, if we should never speak ill otherwise than out of charity, surely most ill-speaking would be cut off; most, I fear, of our tattling about others, much of our gossiping would be marred.

Indeed, so far from bitter or sour our language should be, that it ought to be sweet and pleasant; so far from rough and harsh, that it should be courteous and obliging; so far from signifying wrath, ill-will, contempt, or animosity, that it should express tender affection, good esteem, sincere respect towards our brethren; and be apt to produce the like in them towards us. The sense of them should be grateful to the heart; the very sound and accent of them should be delightful to the ear. Every one should please his neighbour for his good to edification. Our words should always be εν αριτι, with grace, seasoned with salt; they should have the grace of courtesy, they should be seasoned with the salt of discretion, so as to be sweet and savoury to the hearers. Commonly ill language is a certain sign of inward enmity and ill-will. Good-will is wont to show itself in good terms; it clotheth even its grief handsomely, and its displeasure carrieth favour in its face; its rigour is civil and gentle, tempered with pity for the faults and errors which it disliketh, with the desire of their amendment and recovery whom it reprehendeth. It would inflict no more evil than is necessary; it would cure its neighbour's disease without exasperating his patience, troubling his modesty, or impairing his credit. As it always judgeth candidly, so it never condemneth extremely.

II. But so much for the explication of this precept, and the directive part of our discourse. I shall now briefly propound some inducements to the observance thereof.

1. Let us consider that nothing more than railing and reviling is opposite to the nature, and inconsistent with the tenor of our religion; which (as even a heathen did observe of it) *nil nisi justum suadet, et lene,* doth recommend nothing but what is very just and mild; which propoundeth the practices of charity, meekness, pa-

tience, peaceableness, moderation, equity, alacrity, or good humour, as its principal laws, and declareth them the chief fruits of the Divine spirit and grace; which chargeth us to curb and compose all our passions; more particularly to restrain and repress anger, animosity, envy, malice, and such-like dispositions, as the fruits of carnality and corrupt lust; which consequently drieth up all the sources or dammeth up the sluices of bad language. As it doth above all things oblige us to bear no ill-will in our hearts, so it chargeth us to vent none with our mouths.

2. It is therefore often expressly condemned and prohibited as evil. 'Tis the property of the wicked; a character of those who work iniquity, to "whet their tongues like a sword, and bend their bows to shoot their arrows, even bitter words."

3. No practice hath more severe punishments denounced to it than this. The railer (and it is indeed a very proper and fit punishment for him, he being exceedingly bad company) is to be banished out of all good society; thereto St. Paul adjudgeth him: "I have," saith he, "now written unto you, not to keep company, if any man that is called a brother be a fornicator, or covetous, or an idolater, or a railer, or a drunkard, or an extortioner, with such an one not to eat." Ye see what company the railer hath in the text, and with what a crew of people he is coupled; but no good company he is allowed elsewhere; every good Christian should avoid him as a blot, and a pest of conversation; and finally he is sure to be excluded from the blessed society above in heaven; for "neither thieves, nor covetous, nor drunkards, nor revilers, nor extortioners shall inherit the kingdom of God;" and "without" (without the heavenly city) "are dogs," saith St. John in his Revelation; that is, those chiefly who out of currish spite or malignity do frowardly bark at their neighbours, or cruelly bite them with reproachful language.

4. If we look upon such language in its own nature, what is it but a symptom of a foul, a weak, a disordered and a distempered mind? 'Tis the smoke of inward rage and malice: 'tis a stream that cannot issue from a sweet spring; 'tis a storm that cannot bluster out of a calm region. "The words of the pure are pleasant words," as the wise man saith.

5. This practice doth plainly signify low spirit, ill-breeding, and bad manners; and thence misbecometh any wise, any honest, any honourable person. It agreeth to children, who are unapt and unaccustomed to deal in matters considerable, to squabble; to women of meanest rank (apt, by nature, or custom, to be transported with passion) to scold. In our modern languages it is termed villainy, as being proper for rustic boors, or men of coarsest education and employment; who, having their minds debased by being conversant in meanest affairs, do vent their sorry passions, and bicker about their petty concernments, in such strains; who also, being not capable of a fair reputation, or sensible of disgrace to themselves, do little value the credit of others, or care for aspersing it. But such language is unworthy of those persons, and cannot easily be drawn from them, who are wont to exercise their thoughts about nobler matters, who are versed in affairs manageable only by calm deliberation and fair persuasion, not by impetuous and provocative rudeness; which do never work otherwise upon masculine souls than so as to procure disdain and resistance. Such persons, knowing the benefit of a good name, being wont to possess a good repute, prizing their own credit as a considerable good, will never be prone to bereave others of the like by opprobrious speech. A noble enemy will never speak of his enemy in bad terms.

We may further consider that all wise, all honest, all ingenuous persons have an aversion from ill-speaking, and cannot entertain it with any acceptance or complacence; that only ill-natured, unworthy, and naughty people are its willing auditors, or do abet it with applause. The good man, in Psalm xv., *non accipit opprobrium*, doth not take up, or accept, a reproach against his neighbour: "but a wicked doer," saith the wise man, "giveth heed to false lips, and a liar giveth ear to a naughty tongue." And what reasonable man will do that which is disgustful to the wise and good, is grateful only to the foolish and baser sort of men? I pretermit that using this sort of language doth incapacitate a man for benefiting his neighbour, and defeateth his endeavours for his edification, disparaging a good cause, prejudicing the defence of truth, obstructing the effects of good instruction and wholesome reproof; as we did before remark and declare. Further —

6. He that useth this kind of speech doth, as harm and trouble others, so create many great inconveniences and mischiefs to himself thereby. Nothing so inflameth the wrath of men, so provoketh their enmity, so breedeth lasting hatred and spite, as do contumelious words. They are often called swords and arrows; and as such they pierce deeply, and cause most grievous smart; which men feeling are enraged, and accordingly will strive to requite them in the like manner and in all other obvious ways of revenge. Hence strife, clamour, and tumult, care, suspicion, and fear, danger and trouble, sorrow and regret, do seize on the reviler; and he is sufficiently punished for this dealing. No man can otherwise live than in perpetual fear of reciprocal like usage from him whom he is conscious of having so abused. Whence, if not justice, or charity towards others, yet love and pity of ourselves should persuade us to forbear it as disquietful, incommodious, and mischievous to us.

We should indeed certainly enjoy much love, much concord, much quiet, we should live in great safety and security, we should be exempted from much care and fear, if we would restrain ourselves from abusing and offending our neighbour in this kind: being conscious of so just and innocent demeanour towards him, we should converse with him in a pleasant freedom and confidence, not suspecting any bad language or ill usage from him.

7. Hence with evidently good reason is he that useth such language called a fool: and he that abstaineth from it is commended as wise. "A fool's lips enter into contention, and his mouth calleth for strokes. A fool's mouth is his destruction, and his lips are the snare of his soul. He that refraineth his tongue is wise. In the tongue of the wise is health. He that keepeth his lips, keepeth his life: but he that openeth wide his mouth" (that is, in evil-speaking, gaping with clamour and vehemency) "shall have destruction. The words of a wise man's mouth are gracious: but the lips of a fool will swallow up himself. Death and life are in the power of the tongue; and they that love it shall eat the fruit thereof;" that is, of the one or the other, answerably to the kind of speech they choose.

In fine, very remarkable is that advice, or resolution of the grand point concerning the best way of living happily, in the psalmist: "What man is he that desireth life, and loveth many days, that he may see good? Keep thy tongue from evil, and thy lips from speaking guile." Abstinence from ill-speaking he seemeth to propose as the first step towards the fruition of a durably happy life.

8. Lastly, we may consider that it is a grievous perverting of the design of speech, that excellent faculty, which so much distinguisheth us from, so highly advanceth us above other creatures, to use it to the defaming and disquieting of our neighbour. It was given us as an instrument of beneficial commerce and delectable conversation; that with it we might assist and advise, might cheer and comfort one another: we, therefore, in employing it to the disgrace, vexation, damage or prejudice in any kind of our neighbour, do foully abuse it; and so doing, render ourselves indeed worse than dumb beasts: for better far it were that we could say nothing, than that we should speak ill.

"Now the God of grace and peace . . . make us perfect in every good work to do His will, working in us that which is well-pleasing in His sight, through Jesus Christ; to whom be glory for ever and ever. Amen."

THE FOLLY OF SLANDER.

Part 1.

"He that uttereth slander is a fool." — Prov. x. 18.

General declamations against vice and sin are indeed excellently useful, as rousing men to consider and look about them: but they do often want effect, because they only raise confused apprehensions of things, and indeterminate propensions to action; which usually, before men thoroughly perceive or resolve what they should practise, do decay and vanish. As he that cries out "Fire!" doth stir up people, and inspireth them with a kind of hovering tendency every way, yet no man thence to purpose moveth until he be distinctly informed where the mischief is; then do they, who apprehend themselves concerned, run hastily to oppose it: so, till we particularly discern where our offences lie (till we distinctly know the heinous nature and the mischievous consequences of them), we scarce will effectually apply ourselves to correct them. Whence it is requisite that men should be particularly acquainted with their sins, and by proper arguments be dissuaded from them.

In order whereto I have now selected one sin to describe, and dissuade from, being in nature as vile, and in practice as common, as any other whatever that hath prevailed among men. It is slander, a sin which in all times and places hath been epidemical and rife; but which especially doth seem to reign and rage in our age and country.

There are principles innate to men, which ever have, and ever will incline them to this offence. Eager appetites to secular and sensual goods; violent passions, urging the prosecution of what men affect; wrath and displeasure against those who stand in the way of compassing their desires; emulation and envy towards those who happen to succeed better, or to attain a greater share in such things; excessive self-love; unaccountable malignity and vanity, are in some degrees connatural to all men, and ever prompt them to this dealing, as appearing the most efficacious, compendious, and easy way of satisfying such appetites, of promoting such designs, of discharging such passions. Slander thence hath always been a principal engine whereby covetous, ambitious, envious, ill-natured, and vain persons have striven to supplant their competitors, and advance themselves; meaning thereby to procure, what they chiefly prize and like, wealth, or dignity, or reputation, favour and power in the court, respect and interest with the people.

But from especial causes our age peculiarly doth abound in this practice; for, besides the common dispositions inclining thereto, there are conceits newly coined, and greedily entertained by many, which seem purposely levelled at the disparagement of piety, charity, and justice, substituting interest in the room of conscience, authorising and commending for good and wise, all ways serving to private advantage. There are implacable dissensions, fierce animosities, and bitter zeals sprung up; there is an extreme curiosity, niceness, and delicacy of judgment: there is a mighty affectation of seeming wise and witty by any means; there is a great unsettlement of mind, and corruption of manners, generally diffused over people:

from which sources it is no wonder that this flood hath so over-flown, that no banks can restrain it, no fences are able to resist it; so that ordinary conversation is full of it, and no demeanour can be secure from it.

If we do mark what is done in many (might I not say, in most?) companies, what is it but one telling malicious stories of, or fastening odious characters upon another? What do men commonly please themselves in so much, as in carping and harshly censuring, in defaming and abusing their neighbours? Is it not the sport and divertisement of many, to cast dirt in the faces of all they meet with; to bespatter any man with foul imputations? Doth not in every corner a Momus lurk, from the venom of whose spiteful or petulant tongue no eminency of rank, dignity of place, or sacredness of office, no innocence or integrity of life, no wisdom or circumspection in behaviour, no good-nature or benignity in dealing and carriage, can protect any person? Do not men assume to themselves a liberty of telling romances, and framing characters concerning their neighbour, as freely as a poet doth about Hector or Turnus, Thersites or Draucus? Do they not usurp a power of playing with, or tossing about, of tearing in pieces their neighbour's good name, as if it were the veriest toy in the world? Do not many having a form of godliness (some of them, demurely, others confidently, both without any sense of, or remorse for what they do) backbite their brethren? Is it not grown so common a thing to asperse causelessly that no man wonders at it, that few dislike, that scarce any detest it? that most notorious calumniators are heard, not only with patience, but with pleasure; yea, are even held in vogue and reverence as men of a notable talent, and very serviceable to their party? so that slander seemeth to have lost its nature, and not to be now an odious sin, but a fashionable humour, a way of pleasing entertainment, a fine knack, or curious feat of policy; so that no man at least taketh himself or others to be accountable for what is said in this way? Is not, in fine, the case become such, that whoever hath in him any love of truth, any sense of justice or honesty, any spark of charity towards his brethren, shall hardly be able to satisfy himself in the conversations he meeteth; but will be tempted, with the holy prophet, to wish himself sequestered from society, and cast into solitude; repeating those words of his, "Oh, that I had in the wilderness a lodging-place of wayfaring men, that I might leave my people, and go from them: for they are . . . . an assembly of treacherous men, and they bend their tongues like their bow for lies"? This he wished in an age so resembling ours, that I fear the description with equal patness may suit both: "Take ye heed" (said he then, and may we not advise the like now?) "every one of his neighbour, and trust ye not in any brother: for every brother will utterly supplant, and every neighbour will walk with slanders. They will deceive every one his neighbour, and will not speak the truth; they have taught their tongue to speak lies, and weary themselves to commit iniquity."

Such being the state of things, obvious to experience, no discourse may seem more needful, or more useful, than that which serveth to correct or check this practice: which I shall endeavour to do (1) by describing the nature, (2) by declaring the folly of it: or showing it to be very true which the wise man here asserteth, "He that uttereth slander is a fool." Which particulars I hope so to prosecute, that any man shall be able easily to discern, and ready heartily to detest this practice.

I. For explication of its nature, we may describe slander to be the uttering false (or equivalent to false, morally false) speech against our neighbour, in prejudice to his fame, his safety, his welfare, or concernment in any kind, out of malignity, vanity, rashness, ill-nature, or bad design. That which is in Holy Scripture forbidden and reproved under several names and notions: of bearing false witness, false accusation, railing censure, sycophantry, tale-bearing, whispering, backbiting, supplanting, taking up reproach: which terms some of them do signify the nature, others denote the special kinds, others imply the manners, others suggest the ends of this practice. But it seemeth most fully intelligible by observing the several kinds and degrees thereof; as also by reflecting on the divers ways and manners of practising it.

The principal kinds thereof I observe to be these:

1. The grossest kind of slander is that which in the Decalogue is called, bearing false testimony against our neighbour; that is, flatly charging him with facts which he never committed, and is nowise guilty of. As in the case of Naboth, when men were suborned to say,

"Naboth did blaspheme God and the king:" and as was David's case, when he thus complained, "False witnesses did rise up, they laid to my charge things that I knew not of." This kind in the highest way (that is, in judicial proceedings) is more rare; and of all men, they who are detected to practise it, are held most vile and infamous; as being plainly the most pernicious and perilous instruments of injustice, the most desperate enemies of all men's right and safety that can be. But also out of the court there are many knights-errant of the post, whose business it is to run about scattering false reports; sometimes loudly proclaiming them in open companies, sometimes closely whispering them in dark corners; thus infecting conversation with their poisonous breath: these no less notoriously are guilty of this kind, as bearing always the same malice, and sometimes breeding as ill effects.

2. Another kind is, affixing scandalous names, injurious epithets, and odious characters upon persons, which they deserve not. As when Corah and his accomplices did accuse Moses of being ambitious, unjust, and tyrannical: when the Pharisees called our Lord an impostor, a blasphemer, a sorcerer, a glutton and wine-bibber, an incendiary and perverter of the people, one that spake against Cfsar, and forbade to give tribute: when the apostles were charged with being pestilent, turbulent, factious and seditious fellows. This sort being very common, and thence in ordinary repute not so bad, yet in just estimation may be judged, even worse than the former; as doing to our neighbour more heavy and more irreparable wrong. For it imposeth on him really more blame, and that such which he can hardly shake off: because the charge signifieth habit of evil, and includeth many acts; then, being general and indefinite, can scarce be disproved. He, for instance, that calleth a sober man drunkard, doth impute to him many acts of such intemperance (some really past, others probably future), and no particular time or place being specified, how can a man clear himself of that imputation, especially with those who are not thoroughly acquainted with his conversation? So he that calleth a man unjust, proud, perverse, hypocritical, doth load him with most grievous faults, which it is not possible that the most innocent person should discharge himself from.

3. Like to that kind is this: aspersing a man's actions with harsh censures and foul terms, importing that they proceed from ill prin-

ciples, or tend to bad ends; so as it doth not or cannot appear. Thus when we say of him that is generously hospitable, that he is profuse; of him that is prudently frugal, that he is niggardly; of him that is cheerful and free in his conversation, that he is vain or loose; of him that is serious and resolute in a good way, that he is sullen or morose; of him that is conspicuous and brisk in virtuous practice, that it is ambition or ostentation which prompts him; of him that is close and bashful in the like good way, that it is sneaking stupidity, or want of spirit; of him that is reserved, that it is craft; of him that is open, that it is simplicity in him; when we ascribe a man's liberality and charity to vainglory, or popularity; his strictness of life, and constancy, in devotion, to superstition, or hypocrisy. When, I say, we pass such censures, or impose such characters on the laudable or innocent practice of our neighbours, we are indeed slanderers, imitating therein the great calumniator, who thus did slander even God Himself, imputing His prohibition of the fruit unto envy towards men; "God," said he, "doth know that in the day ye eat thereof, your eyes shall be opened, and ye shall be as gods, knowing good and evil;" who thus did ascribe the steady piety of Job, not to a conscientious love and fear of God, but to policy and selfish design: "Doth Job fear God for nought?"

Whoever, indeed, pronounceth concerning his neighbour's intentions otherwise than as they are evidently expressed by words, or signified by overt actions, is a slanderer; because he pretendeth to know, and dareth to aver, that which he nowise possibly can tell whether it be true; because the heart is exempt from all jurisdiction here, is only subject to the government and trial of another world; because no man can judge concerning the truth of such accusations, because no man can exempt or defend himself from them: so that apparently such practice doth thwart all course of justice and equity.

4. Another kind is, perverting a man's words or actions disadvantageously by affected misconstruction. All words are ambiguous, and capable of different senses, some fair, some more foul; all actions have two handles, one that candour and charity will, another that disingenuity and spite may lay hold on; and in such cases to misapprehend is a calumnious procedure, arguing malignant disposition and mischievous design. Thus when two men did witness

that our Lord affirmed, He "could demolish the temple, and rear it again in three days" — although He did indeed speak words to that purpose, meaning them in a figurative sense, discernible enough to those who would candidly have minded His drift and way of speaking — yet they who crudely alleged them against Him are called false witnesses. "At last," saith the Gospel, "came two false witnesses, and said, This fellow said, I am able to destroy the temple," etc. Thus also when some certified of St. Stephen, as having said that "Jesus of Nazareth should destroy that place, and change the customs that Moses delivered;" although probably he did speak words near to that purpose, yet are those men called false witnesses: "And," saith St. Luke, "they set up false witnesses, which said, This man ceaseth not to speak blasphemous words," etc. Which instances plainly do show, if we would avoid the guilt of slander, how careful we should be to interpret fairly and favourably the words and the actions of our neighbour.

5. Another sort of this practice is, partial and lame representation of men's discourse, or their practice; suppressing some part of the truth in them, or concealing some circumstances about them which might serve to explain, to excuse, or to extenuate them. In such a manner easily, without uttering any logical untruth, one may yet grievously calumniate. Thus suppose a man speaketh a thing upon supposition, or with exception, or in way of objection, or merely for disputation sake, in order to the discussion or clearing of truth; he that should report him asserting it absolutely, unlimitedly, positively and peremptorily, as his own settled judgment, would notoriously calumniate. If one should be inveigled by fraud, or driven by violence, or slip by chance into a bad place or bad company, he that should so represent the gross of that accident, as to breed an opinion of that person, that out of pure disposition and design he did put himself there, doth slanderously abuse that innocent person. The reporter in such cases must not think to defend himself by pretending that he spake nothing false; for such propositions, however true in logic, may justly be deemed lies in morality, being uttered with a malicious and deceitful (that is, with a calumnious) mind, being apt to impress false conceits and to produce hurtful effects concerning our neighbour. There are slanderous truths as well as slanderous falsehoods: when truth is uttered with a deceitful heart,

and to a base end, it becomes a lie. "He that speaketh truth," saith the wise man, "showeth forth righteousness: but a false witness deceit." Deceiving is the proper work of slander: and truth abused to that end putteth on its nature, and will engage into like guilt.

6. Another kind of calumny is, by instilling sly suggestions; which although they do not downrightly assert falsehoods, yet they breed sinister opinions in the hearers; especially in those who, from weakness or credulity, from jealousy or prejudice, from negligence or inadvertency, are prone to entertain them. This is done many ways: by propounding wily suppositions, shrewd insinuations, crafty questions, and specious comparisons, intimating a possibility, or inferring some likelihood of, and thence inducing to believe the fact. "Doth not," saith this kind of slanderer, "his temper incline him to do thus? may not his interest have swayed him thereto? had he not fair opportunity and strong temptation to it? hath he not acted so in like cases? Judge you therefore whether he did it not." Thus the close slanderer argueth; and a weak or prejudiced person is thereby so caught, that he presently is ready thence to conclude the thing done. Again: "He doeth well," saith the sycophant, "it is true; but why, and to what end? Is it not, as most men do, out of ill design? may he not dissemble now? may he not recoil hereafter? have not others made as fair a show? yet we know what came of it." Thus do calumnious tongues pervert the judgments of men to think ill of the most innocent, and meanly of the worthiest actions. Even commendation itself is often used calumniously, with intent to breed dislike and ill-will towards a person commended in envious or jealous ears; or so as to give passage to dispraises, and render the accusations following more credible. 'Tis an artifice commonly observed to be much in use there, where the finest tricks of supplanting are practised, with greatest effect; so that *pessimum inimicorum genus, laudantes*; there is no more pestilent enemy than a malevolent praiser. All these kinds of dealing, as they issue from the principles of slander, and perform its work, so they deservedly bear the guilt thereof.

7. A like kind is that of oblique and covert reflections; when a man doth not directly or expressly charge his neighbour with faults, but yet so speaketh that he is understood, or reasonably presumed to do it. This is a very cunning and very mischievous way of slan-

dering; for therein the skulking calumniator keepeth a reserve for himself, and cutteth off from the person concerned the means of defence. If he goeth to clear himself from the matter of such aspersions: "What need," saith this insidious speaker, "of that? must I needs mean you? did I name you? why do you then assume it to yourself? do you not prejudge yourself guilty? I did not, but your own conscience, it seemeth, doth accuse you. You are so jealous and suspicious, as persons overwise or guilty use to be." So meaneth this serpent out of the hedge securely and unavoidably to bite his neighbour, and is in that respect more base and more hurtful than the most flat and positive slanderer.

8. Another kind is that of magnifying and aggravating the faults of others; raising any small miscarriage into a heinous crime, any slender defect into an odious vice, and any common infirmity into a strange enormity; turning a small "mote in the eye" of our neighbour into a huge "beam," a little dimple in his face into a monstrous wen. This is plainly slander, at least in degree, and according to the surplusage whereby the censure doth exceed the fault. As he that, upon the score of a small debt, doth extort a great sum, is no less a thief, in regard to what amounts beyond his due, than if without any pretence he had violently or fraudulently seized on it: so he is a slanderer that, by heightening faults or imperfections, doth charge his neighbour with greater blame, or load him with more disgrace than he deserves. 'Tis not only slander to pick a hole where there is none, but to make that wider which is, so that it appeareth more ugly, and cannot so easily be mended. For charity is wont to extenuate faults, justice doth never exaggerate them. As no man is exempt from some defects, or can live free from some misdemeanours, so by this practice every man may be rendered very odious and infamous.

9. Another kind of slander is, imputing to our neighbour's practice, judgment, or profession, evil consequences (apt to render him odious, or despicable) which have no dependence on them, or connection with them. There do in every age occur disorders and mishaps, springing from various complications of causes, working some of them in a more open and discernible, others in a more secret and subtle way (especially from Divine judgment and providence checking or chastising sin): from such occurrences it is com-

mon to snatch occasion and matter of calumny. Those who are disposed this way, are ready peremptorily to charge them upon whomsoever they dislike or dissent from, although without any apparent cause, or upon most frivolous and senseless pretences; yea, often when reason showeth quite the contrary, and they who are so charged are in just esteem of all men the least obnoxious to such accusations. So usually the best friends of mankind, those who most heartily wish the peace and prosperity of the world and most earnestly to their power strive to promote them, have all the disturbances and disasters happening charged on them by those fiery vixens, who (in pursuance of their base designs, or gratification of their wild passions) really do themselve embroil things, and raise miserable combustions in the world. So it is that they who have the conscience to do mischief, will have the confidence also to disavow the blame and the iniquity, to lay the burden of it on those who are most innocent. Thus, whereas nothing more disposeth men to live orderly and peaceably, nothing more conduceth to the settlement and safety of the public, nothing so much draweth blessings down from heaven upon the commonwealth, as true religion; yet nothing hath been more ordinary than to attribute all the miscarriages and mischiefs that happened unto it; even those are laid at his door, which plainly do arise from the contempt or neglect of it; being the natural fruits or the just punishments of irreligion. King Ahab by forsaking God's commandments, and following wicked superstitions, had troubled Israel, drawing sore judgments and calamities thereon; yet had he the heart and the face to charge those events on the great assertor of piety, Elias: "Art thou he that troubleth Israel?" The Jews by provocation of Divine justice had set themselves in a fair way towards desolation and ruin; this event to come they had the presumption to lay upon the faith of our Lord's doctrine: "If," said they, "we let Him alone, all men will believe on Him, and the Romans shall come, and take away our place and nation:" whereas, in truth, a compliance with His directions and admonitions had been the only means to prevent those presaged mischiefs. And, *si Tibris ascenderit in mfnia*, if any public calamity did appear, then *Christianos ad leones*, Christians must be charged and persecuted as the causes thereof. To them it was that Julian and other pagans did impute all the concussions, confusions, and devastations falling upon the Roman Empire. The sacking of Rome by the Goths they cast upon Christianity; for the vindication of it from which reproach St. Austin did write those renowned books *de Civitate Dei*. So liable are the best and most innocent sort of men to be calumniously accused in this manner.

Another practice (worthily bearing the guilt of slander) is, aiding and being accessory thereto, by anywise furthering, cherishing, abetting it. He that by crafty significations of ill-will doth prompt the slanderer to vent his poison; he that by a willing audience and attention doth readily suck it up, or who greedily swalloweth it down by credulous approbation and assent; he that pleasingly relisheth and smacketh at it, or expresseth a delightful complacence therein: as he is a partner in the fact, so he is a sharer in the guilt. There are not only slanderous throats, but slanderous ears also; not only wicked inventions, which engender and brood lies, but wicked assents, which hatch and foster them. Not only the spiteful mother that conceiveth such spurious brats, but the midwife that helpeth to bring them forth, the nurse that feedeth them, the guardian that traineth them up to maturity, and setteth them forth to live in the world; as they do really contribute to their subsistence, so deservedly they partake in the blame due to them, and must be responsible for the mischief they do. For indeed were it not for such free entertainers, such nourishers, such encouragers of them, slanderers commonly would die in the womb, or prove still-born, or presently entering into the cold air, would expire, or for want of nourishment soon would starve. It is such friends and patrons of them who are the causes that they are so rife; they it is who set ill-natured, base, and designing people upon devising, searching after, and picking up malicious and idle stories. Were it not for such customers, the trade of calumniating would fall. Many pursue it merely out of servility and flattery, to tickle the ears, to soothe the humour, to gratify the malignant disposition or ill-will of others; who upon the least discouragement would give over the practice. If therefore we would exempt ourselves from all guilt of slander, we must not only abstain from venting it, but forbear to regard or countenance it: for "he is," saith the wise man, "a wicked doer who giveth heed to false lips, and a liar who giveth ear to a naughty tongue." Yea, if we thoroughly would be clear from it, we must show an aversion from hearing it, an unwillingness to believe it, an indignation against it;

so either stifling it in the birth, or condemning it to death, being uttered. This is the sure way to destroy it, and to prevent its mischief. If we would stop our ears, we should stop the slanderer's mouth; if we would resist the calumniator, he would fly from us; if we would reprove him, we should repel him. For, "as the north wind driveth away rain, so," the wise man telleth us, "doth an angry countenance a backbiting tongue."

These are the chief and most common kinds of slander; and there are several ways of practising them worthy our observing, that we may avoid them, namely these: —

1. The most notoriously heinous way is, forging and immediately venting ill stories. As it is said of Doeg, "Thy tongue deviseth mischief;" and of another like companion, "Thou givest thy mouth to evil, and thy tongue frameth deceit;" and as our Lord saith of the devil, "When he speaketh a lie, εκ του ιδιων λαλει, he speaketh of his own; for he is a liar, and the father of it." This palpably is the supreme pitch of calumny, incapable of any qualifications or excuse: hell cannot go beyond this; the cursed fiend himself cannot worse employ his wit than in minting wrongful falsehoods.

2. Another way is, receiving from others, and venting such stories, which they who do it certainly know or may reasonably presume to be false; the becoming hucksters of counterfeit wares, or factors in this vile trade. There is no false coiner who hath not some accomplices and emissaries ready to take from his hand and put off his money; and such slanderers at second hand are scarce less guilty than the first authors. He that breweth lies may have more wit and skill, but the broacher showeth the like malice and wickedness. In this there is no great difference between the great devil, that frameth scandalous reports, and the little imps that run about and disperse them.

3. Another way is, when one without competent examination, due weighing, and just reason, doth admit and spread tales prejudicial to his neighbour's welfare; relying for his warrant, as to the truth of them, upon any slight or slender authority. This is a very common and current practice: men presume it lawful enough to say over whatever they hear; to report anything, if they can quote an author for it. "It is not," say they, "my invention; I tell it as I heard

it: *sit fides penes authorem;* let him that informed me undergo the blame if it prove false." So do they conceive themselves excusable for being the instruments of injurious disgrace and damage to their neighbours. But they greatly mistake therein; for as this practice commonly doth arise from the same wicked principles, at least in some degree, and produceth altogether the like mischievous effects, as the wilful devising and conveying slander: so it no less thwarteth the rules of duty, the laws of equity; God hath prohibited it, and reason doth condemn it. "Thou shalt not," saith God in the Law, "go up and down as a tale-bearer among thy people:" as a talebearer (as Rachil, that is), as a merchant or trader in ill reports and stories concerning our neighbour, to his prejudice. Not only the framing of them, but the dealing in them beyond reason or necessity, is interdicted. And it is part of a good man's character in Psalm xv., *Non accipit opprobrium,* "He taketh not up a reproach against his neighbour;" that is, he doth not easily entertain it, much less doth he effectually propagate it: and in our text, "He," it is said, "that uttereth slander" (not only he that conceiveth it) "is a fool."

And in reason, before exact trial and cognisance, to meddle with the fame and interest of another, is evidently a practice full of iniquity, such as no man can allow in his own case, or brook being used towards himself without judging himself to be extremely abused by such reporters. In all reason and equity, yea, in all discretion, before we yield credence to any report concerning our neighbour, or venture to relate it, many things are carefully to be weighed and scanned. We should, concerning our author, consider whether he be not a particular enemy, or disaffected to him: whether he be not ill-humoured, or a delighter in telling bad stories; whether he be not dishonest, or unregardful of justice in his dealings and discourse; whether he be not vain, or careless of what he saith; whether he be not light or credulous, or apt to be imposed upon by any small appearance; whether, at least in the present case, he be not negligent, or too forward and rash in speaking. We should also, concerning the matter reported, mind whether it be possible or probable; whether suitable to the disposition of our neighbour, to his principles, to the constant tenor of his practice; whether the action imputed to him be not liable to misapprehension, or his words to misconstruction. All reason and equity do, I say, exact from us, diligently to consider such things, before we do either embrace ourselves or transmit unto others any story concerning our neighbour; lest unadvisedly we do him irreparable wrong and mischief. Briefly, we should take his case for our own, and consider whether we ourselves should be content that upon like grounds or testimonies any man should believe, or report, disgraceful things concerning us. If we fail to do thus, we do, vainly, or rashly, or maliciously, conspire with the slanderer to the wrong of our innocent neighbour; and that in the psalmist, by a parity of reason, may be transferred to us, "Thou hast consented unto the liar, and hast partaken with the" author of calumny.

4. Of kin to this way is the assenting to popular rumours, and thence affirming matters of obloquy to our neighbour. Every one by experience knows how easily false news do rise, and how nimbly they scatter themselves; how often they are raised from nothing, how soon they from small sparks grow into a great blaze, how easily from one thing they are transformed into another; especially news of this kind, which do suit and feed the bad humour of the vulgar. 'Tis obvious to any man how true that is of Tacitus, how void of consideration, of judgment, of equity, the busy and talking part of mankind is. Whoever therefore gives heed to flying tales, and thrusts himself into the herd of those who spread them, is either strangely injudicious, or very malignantly disposed. If he want not judgment, he cannot but know that when he complieth with popular fame, it is mere chance that he doth not slander, or rather it is odds that he shall do so; he consequently showeth himself to be indifferent whether he doeth it or no, or rather that he doth incline to do it; whence, not caring to be otherwise, or loving to be a slanderer, he in effect and just esteem is such; having at least a slanderous heart and inclination. He that puts it to the venture whether he lieth or no, doth *eo ipso* lie morally, as declaring no care or love of truth. "Thou shalt not," saith the Law, "follow a multitude to do evil;" and with like reason we should not follow the multitude in speaking evil of our neighbour.

5. Another slanderous course is, to build censures and reproaches upon slender conjectures, or uncertain suspicions (those υπονοιαι πονηραι, evil surmises, which St. Paul condemneth). Of these occasion can never be wanting to them who seek them, or are ready to

embrace them; no innocence, no wisdom can anywise prevent them; and if they may be admitted as grounds of defamation, no man's good name can be secure. But he that upon such accounts dareth to asperse his neighbour is in moral computation no less a slanderer than if he did the like out of pure invention, or without any ground at all: for doubtful and false in this case differ little; to devise, and to divine, in matters of this nature, do import near the same. He that will judge or speak ill of others, ought to be well assured of what he thinks or says; he that asserteth that which he doth not know to be true, doth as well lie as he that affirmeth that which he knoweth to be false; for he deceiveth the hearers, begetting in them an opinion that he is assured of what he affirms; especially in dealing with the concernments of others, whose right and repute justice doth oblige us to beware of infringing, charity should dispose us to regard and tender as our own. It is not every possibility, every seeming, every faint show or glimmering appearance, which sufficeth to ground bad opinion or reproachful discourse concerning our brother: the matter should be clear, notorious and palpable, before we admit a disadvantageous conceit into our head, a distasteful resentment into our heart, a harsh word into our mouth about him. Men may fancy themselves sagacious and shrewd, persons of deep judgment and fine wit they may be taken for, when they can dive into others' hearts, and sound their intentions; when through thick mists or at remote distances they can descry faults in them; when they collect ill of them by long trains, and subtle fetches of discourse: but in truth they do thereby rather betray in themselves small love of truth, care of justice, or sense of charity, together with little wisdom and discretion: for truth is only seen in a clear light; justice requireth strict proof. Charity "thinketh no evil," and "believeth all things" for the best; wisdom is not forward to pronounce before full evidence. ("He," saith the wise man, "that answereth a matter before he heareth it, it is folly and shame unto him.") In fine, they who proceed thus, as it is usual that they speak falsely, as it is casual that they ever speak truly, as they affect to speak ill, true or false; so worthily they are to be reckoned among slanderers.

6. Another like way of slandering is, impetuous or negligent sputtering out of words, without minding what truth or consequence there is in them, how they may touch or hurt our neighbour. To

avoid this sin, we must not only be free from intending mischief, but wary of effecting it; not only careful of not wronging one distinct person, but of harming any promiscuously; not only abstinent from aiming directly, but provident not to hit casually any person with obloquy. For as he that dischargeth shot into a crowd, or so as not to look about regarding who may stand in the way, is no less guilty of doing mischief, and bound to make satisfaction to them he woundeth, than if he had aimed at some one person: so if we sling our bad words at random, which may light unluckily, and defame somebody, we become slanderers unawares, and before we think on it. This practice hath not ever all the malice of the worst slander, but it worketh often the effects thereof; and therefore doth incur its guilt, and its punishment; especially it being commonly derived from ill-temper, or from bad habit, which we are bound to watch over, to curb, and to correct. The tongue is a sharp and perilous weapon, which we are bound to keep up in the sheath, or never to draw forth but advisedly, and upon just occasion; it must ever be wielded with caution and care: to brandish it wantonly, to lay about with it blindly and furiously, to slash and smite therewith any that happeneth to come in our way, doth argue malice or madness.

7. It is an ordinary way of proceeding to calumniate, for men, reflecting upon some bad disposition in themselves (although resulting from their own particular temper, from their bad principles, or from their ill custom), to charge it presently upon others; presuming others to be like themselves: like the wicked person in the psalm, "Thou thoughtest that I was altogether such an one as thyself." This is to slander mankind first in the gross; then in retail, as occasion serveth, to asperse any man; this is the way of half-witted Machiavellians, and of desperate reprobates in wickedness, who having prostituted their consciences to vice, for their own defence and solace, would shroud themselves from blame under the shelter of common pravity and infirmity; accusing all men of that whereof they know themselves guilty. But surely there can be no greater iniquity than this, that one man should undergo blame for the ill conscience of another.

These seem to be the chief kinds of slander, and most common ways of practising it. In which description, the folly thereof doth, I suppose, so clearly shine, that no man can look thereon without loathing and despising it, as not only a very ugly, but a most foolish practice. No man surely can be wise who will suffer himself to be defiled therewith. But to render its folly more apparent, we shall display it; declaring it to be extremely foolish upon several accounts. But the doing of this, in regard to your patience, we shall forbear at present.

THE FOLLY OF SLANDER.

Part 2.

"He that uttereth slander is a fool." — Prov. x. 18.

I have formerly in this place, discoursing upon this text, explained the nature of the sin here condemned, with its several kinds and ways of practising.

II. I shall now proceed to declare the folly of it; and to make good by divers reasons the assertion of the wise man, that "He who uttereth slander is a fool."

1. Slandering is foolish, as sinful and wicked.

All sin is foolish upon many accounts; as proceeding from ignorance, error, inconsiderateness, vanity; as implying weak judgment, and irrational choice; as thwarting the dictates of reason, and best rules of wisdom; as producing very mischievous effects to ourselves, bereaving us of the chief goods, and exposing us to the worst evils. What can be more egregiously absurd than to dissent in our opinion and discord in our choice from infinite wisdom; to provoke by our actions sovereign justice, and immutable severity: to oppose almighty power, and offend immense goodness; to render ourselves unlike and contrary in our doings, our disposition, our state, to absolute perfection and felicity? What can be more desperately wild than to disoblige our best Friend, to forfeit His love and favour, to render Him our enemy, who is our Lord and our Judge, upon whose mere will and disposal all our subsistence, all our welfare does absolutely depend? What greater madness can be conceived than to deprive our minds of all true content here, and to separate our souls from eternal bliss hereafter; to gall our consciences now with sore remorse, and to engage ourselves for ever in remediless miseries? Such folly doth all sin include: whence in Scripture style worthily goodness and wisdom are terms equivalent; sin and folly do signify the same thing.

If thence this practice be proved extremely sinful, it will thence sufficiently be demonstrated no less foolish. And that it is extremely sinful may easily be shown. It is the character of the superlatively wicked man: "Thou givest thy mouth to evil, and thy tongue frameth deceit. Thou sittest and speakest against thy brother; thou slanderest thine own mother's son." It is, indeed, plainly the blackest and most hellish sin that can be; that which giveth the grand fiend his names, and most expresseth his nature. He is ὁ διαβολος (the slanderer); Satan, the spiteful adversary; the old snake or dragon, hissing out lies, and spitting forth venom of calumnious accusation; the accuser of the brethren, a murderous, envious, malicious calumniator; the father of lies; the grand defamer of God to man, of man to God, of one man to another. And highly wicked surely must that practice be, whereby we grow namesakes to him, conspire in proceeding with him, resemble his disposition and nature. It is a complication, a comprisal, a collection and sum of all wickedness; opposite to all the principal virtues (to veracity and sincerity, to charity and justice), transgressing all the great commandments, violating immediately and directly all the duties concerning our neighbour.

To lie simply is a great fault, being a deviation from that good rule which prescribeth truth in all our words; rendering us unlike and disagreeable to God, who is the God of truth (who loveth truth, and practiseth it in all His doings, who abominateth all falsehood); including a treacherous breach of faith towards mankind; we being all, in order to the maintenance of society, by an implicit compact, obliged by speech to declare our mind, to inform truly, and not to impose upon our neighbour; arguing pusillanimous timorousness and impotency of mind, a distrust in God's help, and diffidence in all good means to compass our designs; begetting deception and error, a foul and ill-favoured brood: lying, I say, is upon such accounts a sinful and blamable thing; and of all lies those certainly are the worst which proceed from malice or from vanity, or from both, and which work mischief, such as slanders are.

Again, to bear any hatred or ill-will, to exercise enmity towards any man, to design or procure any mischief to our neighbour, whom even Jews were commanded to love as themselves, whose good, by many laws, and upon divers scores, we are obliged to tender as our own, is a heinous fault; and of this apparently the slanderer is most guilty in the highest degree. For evidently true it is which the wise man affirmeth, "A lying tongue hateth those that are afflicted with it;" there is no surer argument of extreme hatred; nothing but the height of ill-will can suggest this practice. The slanderer is an enemy, as the most fierce and outrageous, so the most base and unworthy that can be; he fighteth with the most perilous and most unlawful weapon, in the most furious and foul way that can be. His weapon is an envenomed arrow, full of deadly poison, which he shooteth suddenly, and feareth not: a weapon which by no force can be resisted, by no art declined, whose impression is altogether inevitable and unsustainable. It is a most insidious, most treacherous and cowardly way of fighting; wherein manifestly the weakest and basest spirits have extreme advantage, and may easily prevail against the bravest and worthiest; for no man of honour or honesty can in way of resistance or requital deign to use it, but must infallibly without repugnance be borne down thereby. By it the vile practiser achieveth the greatest mischief that can be. His words are, as the psalmist saith of Doeg, devouring words: "Thou lovest all devouring words, O thou deceitful tongue:" and, "A man," saith the wise man, "that beareth false witness against his neighbour is a maul, and a sword, and a sharp arrow;" that is, he is a complicated instrument of all mischiefs; he smiteth and bruiseth like a maul, he cutteth and pierceth like a sword, he thus doth hurt near at hand; and at a distance he woundeth like a sharp arrow; it is hard anywhere to evade him, or to get out of his reach. "Many," saith another wise man, the imitator of Solomon, "have fallen by the edge of the sword, but not so many as have fallen by the tongue. Well is he that is defended from it, and hath not passed through the venom thereof; who hath not drawn the yoke thereof, nor hath been bound in its bands. For the yoke thereof is a yoke of iron, and the bands thereof are bands of brass. The death thereof is an evil death, the grave were better than it." Incurable are the wounds which the slanderer inflicteth, irreparable the damages which he causeth, indelible the marks which he leaveth. "No balsam can heal the biting of a sycophant;" no thread can stitch up a good name torn by calumnious defamation; no soap is able to cleanse from the stains aspersed by a foul mouth. *Aliquid adhfrebit*; somewhat always of suspicion and ill opinion will stick in the minds of those who have given ear to slander. So extremely opposite is this practice unto the queen of virtues, Charity. Its property indeed is to "believe all things," that is, all things for the best, and to the advantage of our neighbour; not so much as to suspect any evil of him without unavoidably manifest cause; how much more not to devise any falsehood against him! It "covereth" all things, studiously conniving at real defects, and concealing assured miscarriages: how much more not divulging imaginary or false scandals! It disposeth to seek and further any the least good concerning him: how much more will it hinder committing grievous outrage upon his dearest good name!

Again, all injustice is abominable; to do any sort of wrong is a heinous crime; that crime which of all most immediately tendeth to the dissolution of society, and disturbance of human life; which God therefore doth most loathe, and men have reason especially to detest. And of this the slanderer is most deeply guilty. "A witness of Belial scorneth judgment, and the mouth of the wicked devoureth iniquity," saith the wise man. He is indeed, according to just estimation, guilty of all kinds whatever of injury, breaking all the second Table of Commands respecting our neighbour. Most formally and directly he "beareth false witness against his neighbour:" he doth "covet his neighbour's goods;" for 'tis constantly out of such an irregular desire, for his own presumed advantage, to dispossess his neighbour of some good, and transfer it on himself, that the slanderer uttereth his tale: he is ever a thief and robber of his good name, a deflowerer and defiler of his reputation, an assassin and murderer of his honour. So doth he violate all the rules of justice, and perpetrateth all sorts of wrong against his neighbour.

He may, indeed, perhaps conceive it no great matter that he committeth; because he doth not act in so boisterous and bloody a way, but only by words, which are subtle, slim, and transient things: upon his neighbour's credit only, which is no substantial or visible matter. He draweth (thinks he), no blood, nor breaketh any bones, nor impresseth any remarkable scar; 'tis only the soft air he breaketh with his tongue, 'tis only a slight character that he stampeth on the fancy, 'tis only an imaginary stain that he daubeth his neighbour with; therefore he supposeth no great wrong done, and seemeth to himself innocent, or very excusable. But these conceits arise from great inconsiderateness, or mistake: nor can they excuse the slanderer from grievous injustice. For in dealing with our neighbour, and meddling with his property, we are not to value things according to our fancy, but according to the price set on them by the owner; we must not reckon that a trifle, which he prizeth as a jewel. Since, then, all men (especially men of honour and honesty) do, from a necessary instinct of nature, estimate their good name beyond any of their goods—yea, do commonly hold it more dear and precious than their very lives—we, by violently or fraudulently bereaving them of it, do them no less wrong than if we should rob or cozen them of their substance; yea, than if we should maim their body, or spill their blood, or even stop their breath. If they as grievously feel it, and resent it as deeply, as they do any other outrage, the injury is really as great, to them. Even the slanderer's own judgment and conscience might tell him so much; for they who most slight another's fame, are usually very tender of their own, and can with no patience endure that others should touch it; which demonstrates the inconsiderateness of their judgment, and the iniquity of their practice. It is an injustice not to be corrected or cured. Thefts may be restored, wounds may be cured; but there is no restitution or cure of a lost good name: it is therefore an irreparable injury.

Nor is the thing itself, in true judgment, contemptible; but in itself really very considerable. "A good name," saith Solomon himself (no fool), "is rather to be chosen than great riches; and loving favour rather than silver and gold." In its consequences it is much more so; the chief interests of a man, the success of his affairs, his ability to do good (for himself, his friends, his neighbour), his safety, the best comforts and conveniences of his life, sometimes his life itself, depending thereon; so that whoever doth snatch or filch it from him, doth not only according to his opinion, and in moral value, but in real effect commonly rob, sometimes murder, ever exceedingly wrong his neighbour. It is often the sole reward of a man's virtue and all the fruit of his industry; so that by depriving him of that, he is robbed of all his estate, and left stark naked of all, excepting a good conscience, which is beyond the reach of the world, and which no malice or misfortune can divest him of. Full then of iniquity, full of uncharitableness, full of all wickedness is this practice; and consequently full it is of folly. No man, one would think, of any tolerable sense, should dare or deign to incur the guilt of a practice so vile and base, so indeed diabolical and detestable. But further more particularly —

2. The slanderer is plainly a fool, because he maketh wrong judgments and valuations of things, and accordingly driveth on silly bargains for himself, in result whereof he proveth a great loser. He means by his calumnious stories either to vent some passion boiling in him, or to compass some design which he affects, or to please some humour that he is possessed with: but is any of these things worth purchasing at so dear a rate? can there be any valuable exchange for our honesty? Is it not more advisable to suppress our passion, or to let it evaporate otherwise, than to discharge it in so foul a way? Is it not better to let go a petty interest, than to further it by committing so notorious and heinous a sin; to let an ambitious project sink, than to buoy it up by such base means? Is it not wisdom rather to smother or curb our humour, than by satisfying it thus to forfeit our innocence? Can anything in the world be so considerable, that for its sake we should defile our souls by so foul a practice, making shipwreck of a good conscience, abandoning honour and honesty, incurring all the guilt and all the punishment due to so enormous a crime? Is it not far more wisdom, contentedly to see our neighbour to enjoy credit and success, to flourish and thrive in the world, than by such base courses to sully his reputation, to rifle him of his goods, to supplant or cross him in his affairs? We do really, when we think thus to depress him, and to climb up to wealth or credit by the ruins of his honour, but debase ourselves. Whatever comes of it, whether he succeeds or is disappointed therein, assuredly he that useth such courses will himself be the greatest loser, and deepest sufferer. 'Tis true which the wise man saith, "The getting of treasures by a lying tongue, is a vanity tossed to and fro

of them that seek death." And, "Woe unto them," saith the prophet, "that draw iniquity with cords of vanity;" that is, who by falsehood endeavour to compass unjust designs.

But it is not, perhaps he will pretend, to assuage a private passion, or to promote his particular concernment, that he makes so bold with his neighbour, or deals so harshly with him; but for the sake of orthodox doctrine, for advantage of the true Church, for the advancement of public good, he judgeth it expedient to asperse him. This indeed is the covert of innumerable slanders: zeal for some opinion, or some party, beareth out men of sectarian and factious spirits in such practices; they may do, they may say anything for those fine ends. What is a little truth, what is any man's reputation in comparison to the carrying on such brave designs? But (to omit that men do usually prevaricate in these cases; that it is not commonly for love of truth, but of themselves; not so much for the benefit of their sect, but for their own interest, that they calumniate) this plea will nowise justify such practice. For truth and sincerity, equity and candour, meekness and charity are inviolably to be observed, not only towards dissenters in opinion, but even towards declared enemies of truth itself; we are to bless them (that is, to speak well of them, and to wish well to them), not to curse them (that is, not to reproach them, or to wish them ill, much less to belie them). Truth also, as it cannot ever need, so doth it always loathe and scorn the patronage and the succour of lies; it is able to support and protect itself by fair means; it will not be killed upon a pretence of saving it, or thrive by its own ruin. Nor indeed can any party be so much strengthened and underpropped, as it will be weakened and undermined by such courses. No cause can stand firm upon a bottom so loose and slippery as falsehood is. All the good a slanderer can do is, to disparage what he would maintain. In truth, no heresy can be worse than that would be which should allow to play the devil in any case. He that can dispense with himself to slander a Jew or a Turk, doth in so doing render himself worse than either of them by profession is: for even they, and even pagans themselves, disallow the practice of inhumanity and iniquity. All men by light of nature avow truth to be honourable, and faith to be indispensably observed. He doth not understand what it is to be Christian, or careth not to practise according thereto, who can find in his heart in any case, upon any pretence, to calumniate. In fine, to prostitute our conscience, or sacrifice our honesty, for any cause, to any interest whatever, can never be warrantable or wise. Further—

3. The slanderer is a fool, because he useth improper means and preposterous methods of effecting his purposes. As there is no design worth the carrying on by ways of falsehood and iniquity, so is there scarce any, no good or lawful one at least, which may not more surely, more safely, more cleverly be achieved by means of truth and justice. Is not always the straight way more short than the oblique and crooked? is not the plain way more easy than the rough and cragged? is not the fair way more pleasant and passable than the foul? Is it not better to walk in paths that are open and allowed, than in those that are shut up and prohibited, than to clamber over walls, to break through fences, to trespass upon enclosures? Surely yes: "He that walketh uprightly, walketh surely." Using strict veracity and integrity, candour and equity, is the best method of accomplishing good designs. Our own industry, good use of the parts and faculties God hath given us, embracing fair opportunities, God's blessing and providence, are sufficient means to rely upon for procuring, in an honest way, whatever is convenient for us. These are ways approved, and amiable to all men; they procure the best friends, and fewest enemies; they afford to the practises a cheerful courage, and good hope; they meet with less disappointment, and have no regret or shame attending them. He that hath recourse to the other base means, and "maketh lies his refuge," as he renounceth all just and honest means, as he disclaimeth all hope in God's assistance, and forfeiteth all pretence to His blessing: so he cannot reasonably expect good success, or be satisfied in any undertaking. The supplanting way indeed seems the most curt and compendious way of bringing about dishonest or dishonourable designs: but as good design is certainly dishonoured thereby, so is it apt thence to be defeated; it raises up enemies and obstacles, yielding advantages to whoever is disposed to cross us. As in trade it is notorious that the best course to thrive is by dealing squarely and truly; any fraud or cozenage appearing there doth overthrow a man's credit, and drive away custom from him: so in all other transactions, as he that dealeth justly and fairly will have his affairs proceed roundly, and shall find men ready to comply with him, so

he that is observed to practise falsehood will be declined by some, opposed by others, disliked by all: no man scarce willingly will have to do with him; he is commonly forced to stand out in business, as one that plays foul play.

4. Lastly, the slanderer is a very fool, as bringing many great inconveniences, troubles, and mischiefs on himself.

First, "A fool's mouth," saith the wise man, "is his destruction, his lips are the snare of his soul:" and if any kind of speech is destructive and dangerous, then is this certainly most of all; for by no means can a man inflame so fierce anger, impress so stiff hatred, raise so deadly enmity against himself, and consequently so endanger his safety, ease and welfare, as by this practice. Men can more easily endure, and sooner will forgive, any sort of abuse than this; they will rather pardon a robber of their goods, than a defamer of their good name.

Secondly, such an one indeed is not only odious to the person immediately concerned, but generally to all men that observe his practice; every man presently will be sensible how easily it may be his own case, how liable he may be to be thus abused, in a way against which there is no guard or defence. The slanderer therefore is apprehended a common enemy, dangerous to all men; and thence rendereth all men averse from him, and ready to cross him. Love and peace, tranquillity and security can only be maintained by innocent and true dealing: so the psalmist hath well taught us: "What man is he that desireth life, and loveth many days, that he may see good? Keep thy tongue from evil, and thy lips from speaking guile."

Thirdly, all wise, all noble, all ingenuous and honest persons have an aversion from this practice, and cannot entertain it with any acceptance or complacence. "A righteous man hateth lying," saith the wise man. It is only ill-natured and ill-nurtured, unworthy and naughty people that are willing auditors or encouragers thereof. "A wicked doer," saith the wise man again, "giveth heed to false lips; and a liar giveth ear to a naughty tongue." All love of truth and regard to justice, and sense of humanity, all generosity and ingenuity, all charity and good-will to men, must be extinct in those who can with delight, or indeed with patience, lend an ear or give any countenance to a slanderer: and is not he a very fool who chooseth to displease the best, only soothing the worst of men?

Fourthly, the slanderer indeed doth banish himself from all conversation and company, or intruding into it becomes very disgustful thereto; for he worthily is not only looked upon as an enemy to those whom he slandereth, but to those also upon whom he obtrudeth his calumnious discourse. He not only wrongeth the former by the injury, but he mocketh the latter by the falsehood of his stories; implicitly charging his hearers with weakness and credulity, or with injustice and pravity.

Fifthly, he also derogateth wholly from his own credit in all matters of discourse. For he that dareth thus to injure his neighbour, who can trust him in anything he speaks? what will not he say to please his vile humour, or further his base interest? what, thinks any man, will he scruple or boggle at, who hath the heart in thus doing wrong and mischief to imitate the devil? Further—

Sixthly, this practice is perpetually haunted with most troublesome companions, inward regret and self-condemnation, fear and disquiet: the conscience of dealing so unworthily doth smite and rack him; he is ever in danger, and thence in fear to be discovered, and requited for it. Of these passions the manner of his behaviour is a manifest indication: for men do seldom vent their slanderous reports openly and loudly, to the face or in the ear of those who are concerned in them; but do utter them in a low voice, in dark corners, out of sight and hearing, where they conceit themselves at present safe from being called to an account. "Swords," saith the psalmist of such persons, "are in their lips: Who (say they) doth hear?" And, "Whoso privily slandereth his neighbour, him will I cut off," saith David again, intimating the common manner of this practice. Calumny is like "the plague, that walketh in darkness." Hence appositely are the practisers thereof termed whisperers and backbiters: their heart suffers them not openly to avow, their conscience tells them they cannot fairly defend their practice. Again—

Seventhly, the consequence of this practice is commonly shameful disgrace, with an obligation to retract and render satisfaction: for seldom doth calumny pass long without being detected and confuted. "He that walketh uprightly, walketh surely: but he that perverteth his ways shall be known:" and, "The lip of truth shall be established for ever; but a lying lip is but for a moment," saith the great observer of things. And when the slander is disclosed, the slanderer is obliged to excuse (that is, to palliate one lie with another, if he can do it), or forced to recant, with much disgrace and extreme displeasure to himself: he is also many times constrained, with his loss and pain, to repair the mischief he hath done.

Eighthly, to this in likelihood the concernments of men, and the powers which guard justice, will forcibly bring him; and certainly his conscience will bind him thereto; God will indispensably exact it from him. He can never have any sound quiet in his mind, he can never expect pardon from Heaven, without acknowledging his fault, repairing the wrong he hath done, restoring that good name of which he dispossessed his neighbour: for in this no less than in other cases conscience cannot be satisfied, remission will not be granted, except due restitution be performed; and of all restitutions this surely is the most difficult, most laborious, and most troublesome. 'Tis nowise so hard to restore goods stolen or extorted, as to recover a good opinion lost, to wipe off aspersions cast on a man's name, to cure a wounded reputation: the most earnest and diligent endeavour can hardly ever effect this, or spread the plaster so far as the sore hath reached. The slanderer therefore doth engage himself into great straits, incurring an obligation to repair an almost irreparable mischief.

Ninthly, this practice doth also certainly revenge itself, imposing on its actor a perfect retaliation; "a tooth for a tooth;" an irrecoverable infamy to himself, for the infamy he causeth to others. Who will regard his fame, who will be concerned to excuse his faults, who so outrageously abuseth the reputation of others? He suffereth justly, he is paid in his own coin, will any man think, who doth hear him reproached.

Tenthly, in fine, the slanderer, if he doth not, by serious and sore repentance retract his practice, doth banish himself from heaven and happiness, doth expose himself to endless miseries and sorrows. For, if none that "maketh a lie shall enter into the heavenly city;" if without those mansions of joy and bliss "every one" must eternally abide "that loveth or maketh a lie;" if πασι τοις ψευδεαι, "to all liars their portion" is assigned "in the lake which burneth with fire and brimstone;" then assuredly the capital liar, the slanderer, who lieth most injuriously and mischievously, shall be far excluded from felicity, and thrust down into the depth of that miserable place. If, as St. Paul saith, no "railer," or evil-speaker, "shall inherit the kingdom of God," how far thence shall they be removed who without any truth or justice do speak ill of and reproach their neighbour? If for every αργον ρημα, "idle," or vain, "word" we must "render a" strict "account," how much more shall we be severely reckoned with for this sort of words, so empty of truth and void of equity: words that are not only negatively vain, or useless, but positively vain, as false and spoken to bad purpose? If slander perhaps here may evade detection, or escape deserved punishment, yet infallibly hereafter, at the dreadful day, it shall be disclosed, irreversibly condemned, inevitably persecuted with condign reward of utter shame and sorrow.

Is not he then, he who, out of malignity, or vanity, to serve any design, or soothe any humour in himself or others, doth by committing this sin involve himself in all these great evils, both here and hereafter, a most desperate and deplorable fool?

Having thus described the nature of this sin, and declared the folly thereof, we need, I suppose, to say no more for dissuading it; especially to persons of a generous and honest mind, who cannot but scorn to debase and defile themselves by so mean and vile a practice; or to those who seriously do profess Christianity, that is, the religion which peculiarly above all others prescribeth constant truth, strictest justice, and highest charity.

I shall only add, that since our faculty of speech (wherein we do excel all other creatures) was given us, as in the first place to praise and glorify our Maker, so in the next to benefit and help our neighbour; as an instrument of mutual succour and delectation, of friendly commerce and pleasant converse together; for instructing and advising, comforting and cheering one another: it is an unnatural perverting, and an irrational abuse thereof, to employ it to the damage, disgrace, vexation, or wrong in any kind of our brother. Better indeed had we been as brutes without its use, than we are, if so worse than brutishly we abuse it.

Finally, all these things being considered, we may, I think, reasonably conclude it most evidently true that "He which uttereth slander is a fool."